GOD'S CRANKY PROPHETS: JONAH & HABAKKUK

*A Bible Study on Responding in Faith When
You Don't Like What God Is Doing*

MARCI OGROSKY

WESTBOW®
PRESS
A DIVISION OF THOMAS NELSON
& ZONDERVAN

Scripture quotations are from The Holy Bible, English Standard Version' (ESV'), copyright ©2001 by Crossway, a publishing ministry of Good News Publishers. Used by permission. All rights reserved.

WestBow Press books may be ordered through booksellers or by contacting:

WestBow Press
A Division of Thomas Nelson & Zondervan
1663 Liberty Drive
Bloomington, IN 47403
www.westbowpress.com
1 (866) 928-1240

ISBN: 978-1-4908-5428-1 (sc)
ISBN: 978-1-4908-5429-8 (e)

Library of Congress Control Number: 2014917508

Printed in the United States of America.

WestBow Press rev. date: 11/19/2014

Contents

THE *Faith* TRILOGY

A BIBLE STUDY SERIES BY MARCI OGROSKY

Also available in the series:
Looking to Christ: The Book of Hebrews

❧ Introduction ❧

If we are honest, we have to admit there are times we don't understand or like the way God runs the world. His ways do not always make sense to us. We know that God is perfectly good and just, yet sometimes it appears that He allows wickedness to prosper and go unpunished.

It frustrates us when we cry out to God for justice but He does not seem to hear or care. You might be pleading with the Lord for justice regarding personal matters in your family or at work. It could be that you are crying out against oppression of the poor, religious persecution, government corruption, or global wars. Perhaps you question why God allows innocent people to suffer.

Scripture reminds us we are not alone in our distress. The Old Testament prophets Jonah and Habakkuk faced the same dilemma long ago. They lived in separate kingdoms one hundred fifty years apart in time and they were called by God to address different circumstances, but what they shared in common was a passion for the holiness, goodness and justice of God. They also shared frustration that God seemed to tolerate evil.

Jonah and Habakkuk each struggled to find a satisfactory theodicy, meaning a justification or explanation of God's actions with regard to evil in light of His goodness.[1] Jonah was especially troubled by the tension between divine justice and mercy. He resented God's compassion for the wicked people of Nineveh, Assyria, and angrily refused to conform his will to God's:

> "I knew that you are a gracious God and merciful, slow to
> anger and abounding in steadfast love, and relenting from disaster.

> Therefore now, O LORD... it is better for me to die than to live."
> (Jonah 4:2-3 ESV)

Habakkuk's initial complaint was related to God's failure to punish sin among His own people in Judah:

> "O LORD, how long shall I cry for help, and
> you will not hear... you will not save... you idly look at wrong?"
> (Habakkuk 1:2-3)

However, when God revealed His plan to punish Judah by means of the wicked Babylonians, Habakkuk complained to God about His unfair methods. The candor of the prophets' complaints makes us a bit uneasy because our sovereign God does not have to explain His ways to us. Is it really all right to tell Him we don't like the way He runs the world?

Jonah and Habakkuk show us that being in a personal, covenant relationship with God means that our prayers can be honest because He is gracious. But there is more. When we complain to God we should approach Him with a teachable heart. Our goal must not be to get our own way, but to seek God's counsel and learn from Him. We should develop right feelings and will (orthopathy) so that our hearts are aligned with God.

God does care about injustice and deals with it in His own sovereign and gracious way. We are to trust God's character and saving purposes, responding in obedience to His call on our lives. Whether or not we understand or like the way God is working in our life and the world, His redemptive purposes are always good and will not fail. Because God has fulfilled His redemptive purposes in Jesus Christ, we can have confidence that God can be trusted for all aspects of life including matters of justice.

In the end neither Jonah nor Habakkuk got the answers they wanted from God. Jonah's response was to become increasingly angry, refusing to accept God's right to act as He pleases. Habakkuk, though, faithfully yielded to God's sovereignty. We are to imitate Habakkuk by trusting and submitting to God even when we do not like what He is doing. Like Habakkuk, our complaints should turn into praise in every circumstance:

"Though the fig tree should not blossom,
nor fruit be on the vines,
the produce of the olive fail
and the fields yield no food,
the flock be cut off from the fold
and there be no herd in the stalls,
yet I will rejoice in the LORD;
I will take joy in the God of my salvation."
(Habakkuk 3:17-18)

This study guide is designed for group or individual Bible study. The lessons provide background information, related Scripture references, and study questions to deepen the reader's understanding of the Bible passage along with its application to our lives. There are six sets of study questions per lesson, making it easier to study the lesson a little at a time during a week. A leader's guide and other appendices are provided near the end of the book.

The prayers throughout the study guide come from John Calvin's 16th century *Commentary* on the prophets. Calvin was a leading figure in the Protestant Reformation. Each of these pastoral prayers is actually one very long sentence that has been modified in form to make it easier for modern readers. Enjoy these timeless meditations from one of the Reformation's most profound theologians.

May this study of Jonah and Habakkuk, two of God's cranky but beloved prophets, encourage you to take your concerns to God and allow Him to transform your will so that it is aligned with His in all circumstances.

SECTION I

THE PROPHET JONAH

❧ Lesson 1 ❧
The Role of Old Testament Prophets
Luke 24:25-27, 44-49

Welcome to this study of God's cranky Old Testament prophets, Jonah and Habakkuk. Before we look at the prophet Jonah, we will begin with a general overview of Old Testament prophets.

Part I: Setting the Stage

Purpose
This lesson explores the big picture of Old Testament prophets and prophecy in order to lay the groundwork for studying Jonah and Habakkuk in more detail in the coming lessons. It is important to understand that the role of an Old Testament prophet was to be God's spokesperson and representative.

Look for the following application points in this lesson:

1. God revealed His redemptive purposes through His representatives, the Old Testament prophets, and ultimately through Jesus Christ.
2. Some prophecies were conditional and others were unconditional.
3. God continues to speak to us today through the writings of the prophets.

Jesus' Bible
Jesus told His disciples that the whole of Scriptures testified to Him as the Messiah. The Scriptures at that time referred to the Hebrew Bible, known to us as the Old Testament. This was Jesus' Bible. Jews call it the

Mikra ("that which is read") or Tanakh. Tanakh is an acronym of three consonants (TNK) that stand for the three parts of the Hebrew Bible, as explained below.

Torah (the Law): This is often called the Pentateuch by Christians. It consists of the first five books of the Bible: Genesis, Exodus, Leviticus, Numbers and Deuteronomy.

Naviim (the Prophets): This includes the Former Prophets (Joshua, Judges, Samuel and Kings) and Latter Prophets (the writing prophets except Daniel).

Ketuvim (the Writings): This includes Psalms, Daniel and the rest of the books of the Old Testament.

The Writing Prophets
Look at the Table of Contents in your Bible to see where Jonah and Habakkuk fit into the Old Testament. You'll find a group of writings by sixteen prophets starting with Isaiah. These prophets lived during a five-hundred year period from the divided kingdom until after the Babylonian Exile. Based largely on the length of their books, the first four prophets are called major prophets and the next twelve are minor. As you can see in the chart below, Jonah and Habakkuk are two of the minor prophets.

The Writing Prophets

<u>Major</u>	<u>Minor</u>		
Isaiah	Hosea	Jonah	Zephaniah
Jeremiah	Joel	Micah	Haggai
Ezekiel	Amos	Nahum	Zechariah
Daniel	Obadiah	Habakkuk	Malachi

Other Prophets
Besides the writing prophets there are other prophets in the Old Testament like Moses, Miriam, Deborah, Samuel, Elijah, Elisha, Huldah, Nathan, Shemaiah, Micaiah, and more.[2] Some of their sayings are preserved in various places in the Bible, but others are no longer in existence or were never written down.

Many people consider the last prophet in the tradition of Old Testament prophets not to be Malachi but John the Baptist. John appears in the New Testament preaching a message of repentance four hundred years after Malachi. John prepared the way for the Messiah and announced the arrival of the Lord Jesus Christ in fulfillment of Old Testament messianic prophecy.

Prophetic Messages
The prophets were chosen by God to speak on His behalf to the people and their leaders. Prophets were called to *forthtell* and proclaim God's word as well as to *foretell* and predict. They spoke out against injustice, false worship and covenant violations. They called for repentance and reform as they warned of God's future judgment. There was also the promise of God's glorious salvation and restoration through the Messiah after the punishment of exile.

Since a key role of the prophets was to prepare and point God's people forward to His plan of salvation through the promised Messiah, the arrival of the Messiah meant that the role of Old Testament prophet was no longer necessary. The prophets' writings, though, are a lasting testimony to God's redemptive purposes. Those of us who live in the era of fulfillment of messianic prophecy in Jesus Christ are to be truly grateful for the faithful witness of the prophets.

Part II: Studying Scripture

1. True Prophets

a) God's prophets were known by several terms that reflect various functions. What common terms for Old Testament prophets are found in the following passages?

I Samuel 3:20 _____

I Samuel 9:6 _____

I Samuel 9:9 _____

Hosea 9:8 _____

Amos 3:7 _____

Malachi 3:1 _____

b) The usual term for a prophet was *navi* ("called one"). A *navi* was chosen by God to be His spokesperson, delivering the words God gave him or her. Prophets were compelled by the Holy Spirit to speak what God told them and were not at liberty to withhold God's word, no matter what the cost. Read Jeremiah 20:8-9. What happened to Jeremiah when he preached? What happened when he tried to refrain from preaching God's word?

c) The bulk of written prophecy consists of speeches made by the prophets. Prophets delivered oracles of judgment and salvation, parables, laments, praises, warnings, arguments, blessings, and lawsuits. A few prophets were called by God to act out His message in dramatic and memorable ways. Read Ezekiel 4:1-4. The Babylonian siege of Jerusalem led to its destruction in 586 B.C. How was Ezekiel supposed to symbolically act out the coming judgment against Jerusalem? Who does Ezekiel represent in the drama?

2. False Prophets

Read I Kings 22:1-9, 17-18, 28-36

As the monarchy developed in Israel there also arose the formal office of paid prophet. Prophets on the king's payroll were false prophets who usually said what the king wanted to hear. The king and his paid prophets often resented God's prophets who opposed them.

When King Ahab of Israel wanted to know if he could successfully wage war against Syria, he consulted four hundred of his paid prophets. They all predicted victory. King Jehoshaphat of Judah planned to join Ahab, but first he insisted that Ahab consult a true prophet of the Lord.

a) In v. 8, why was Ahab reluctant to consult God's prophet Micaiah?

b) In v. 17-18, what did Micaiah prophesy, just as Ahab feared?

c) One way to discern if a prophet was false was to see whether or not the prophecy came to pass. In v. 35-36, whose prophecy came true, that of Micaiah or the paid prophets?

3. Conditional Prophecies

Read Jeremiah 18:7-12

Prophecies of judgment and blessing were generally conditional. That means the outcome of what was prophesied could be delayed or reversed by God, depending on such factors as whether people repented or hardened their hearts against Him. This conditional aspect of prophecy helps explain why it sometimes seems that God changes His mind or fails to keep a promise in Scripture, even though we know He cannot lie. We will come across conditional prophecy in the book of Jonah.

a) In v. 11, what does God intend to do against the nation of Judah because of their sin? What condition does He state that could alter the outcome?

b) In v. 12, how does Judah respond, leading to destruction and exile?

c) Think about how you respond when you are confronted with your own sin. Do you tend to get defensive and harden your heart toward God's word, or do you turn from sin in repentance? How will you learn to soften your heart to accept godly correction?

4. Unconditional Prophecies

Read Luke 24:25-27

Messianic prophecies were unconditional and had to be fulfilled. Unlike prophecies of judgment and blessing, there were no conditions or contingencies that could alter the outcome of messianic prophecies. Christians should understand that these prophecies predicted the necessity and purpose of Jesus' suffering, death and resurrection.

On the evening of Jesus' resurrection He appeared to two disciples on the road to Emmaus. The travelers were trying to make sense of recent events: Jesus' crucifixion, the empty tomb, and the angels' message that Jesus was alive. God evidently prevented them from recognizing the risen Jesus right away.

a) In v. 25, what does Jesus say about the disciples? In what ways does His rebuke apply to you as well? What heart changes do you need to make?

b) In v. 26-27, what does Jesus say about Himself? Which parts of Scripture does Jesus rely on to explain Himself? Evangelist Charles H. Spurgeon says the two disciples experienced "heavenly heartburn" while Jesus taught them:

> "They were willing to learn. Never better pupils, never a better Teacher, never a better school book, never a better explanation! ...Pray the Lord to enlighten *you!*"[3]

c) Read Isaiah 52:13-53:12. This is Isaiah's fourth Servant song, one of the best known prophecies about the Messiah's suffering. Isaiah foretold that the future Messiah, God's Suffering Servant, would suffer in place of God's people so they might have eternal life. Isaiah speaks of double imputation wherein their sin is imputed to Christ and His righteousness is imputed to them. What is your response to Christ's suffering in your place? How does it strengthen your faith to know that God laid out His plan of salvation well in advance of Christ's coming? What steps will you take to become more familiar with messianic prophecies such as Isaiah's?

5. Continuity

There was consistency and continuity among true prophets throughout the centuries. Even when prophetic messages contained new revelation from God, such revelation was always consistent with Mosaic Law. The prophets built on the messages of previous prophets, sometimes borrowing words from them.

The Old Testament carries over to the New Testament in significant ways. The theological views in the Old Testament with regard to God, humanity, covenant, election, and judgment underlie the theology of Jesus, His disciples, and the writings of the New Testament. Although in a sense the gospel was something entirely new, it was also a continuation of God's plan of salvation.

a) Read Isaiah 40:3 and Malachi 3:1. Malachi, the last writing prophet in the Old Testament, quotes the prophet Isaiah who wrote centuries earlier. What do Malachi and Isaiah predict about the LORD's messenger?

b) Read Malachi 4:5-6. This is the last prophecy of the Old Testament. Who does Malachi identify as the LORD's messenger?

c) Read Matthew 11:7-14. Jesus indicates that Malachi and Isaiah's prophecies have been fulfilled. Jesus the Lord has come, ushering in the kingdom of heaven in spite of the world's opposition. Who is the messenger that acted as Elijah and prepared the way of the Lord by preaching repentance?

d) Read John 1:29-34. John the Baptist recognized that Jesus was the expected Messiah and that John's own role as messenger had been completed. What two titles does John the Baptist call Jesus and what is the significance of each one?[4] Are you willing to call Jesus by these titles? What do you need to do to surrender your life to Jesus more completely?

6. Our Part

Read Luke 24:44-49

The travelers on the road to Emmaus finally recognized Jesus and rushed back to Jerusalem to tell the apostles and others the good news that Jesus was indeed alive. It turned out that the apostle Simon Peter had also met the risen Jesus that day. As the group was talking, Jesus suddenly appeared among them.

a) In v. 44, which parts of Scripture does Jesus rely on to explain Himself?

b) In v. 46, what aspect of messianic prophecy has Jesus already fulfilled?

c) In v. 47-48, what aspect of messianic prophecy is Jesus still fulfilling through His body, the church?

d)   As part of Christ's body, you are empowered by the indwelling Holy Spirit to spread the message of repentance and forgiveness of sins available in Christ. This is not an optional activity. This part of messianic prophecy can only be fulfilled by the church and it must be fulfilled. How are you doing at participating in this mission? What will you do to participate more fully?

Part III: Personal Application and Growth

Today's lesson points to several important truths that apply to our personal lives. Allow these truths to penetrate your mind, soften your heart, deepen your faith and affect your behavior to help you continually grow in Christ.

1.   God revealed His redemptive purposes through His representatives, the Old Testament prophets, and ultimately through Jesus Christ.

By God's grace alone, Jesus Christ came into the world to accomplish salvation as foretold by the prophets. How will you express your gratitude to God today for this amazing, undeserved gift of salvation? What difference will an attitude of gratitude make in the way you approach everyday life?

2.   Some prophecies were conditional and others were unconditional.

When a prophecy of judgment did not come true it did not mean God failed to keep a promise, but that His conditions were met or He was merciful. God's word is always trustworthy. How will you apply your confidence in the reliability of God's word to the way you read the Bible?

3.   God continues to speak to us today through the writings of the prophets.

One of the messages proclaimed by the prophets and by Jesus was a call to repent (Ezekiel 14:6; Mark 1:15). It is still a relevant message for us.

What is one area where you are in rebellion against God and His word? What change are you willing to make this week to turn toward God in repentance?

Part IV: Closing Prayer

by John Calvin

Grant, Almighty God, that since we are at this day as guilty before you as the Israelites of old were, who were so rebellious against your prophets, and as you have often tried sweetly to allure us to yourself without any success, and as we have not thus far ceased, by our continual obstinacy, to provoke your wrath;

O grant, that being moved at last by the warnings you give us, we may prostrate ourselves before your face and not wait until you put forth your hand to destroy us, but, on the contrary, strive to consider your judgment;

And that being at the same time surely convinced that you are ready to be reconciled to us in Christ, we may flee to Him as our mediator;

And that relying on His intercession, we may not doubt that you are ready to give us pardon, until having at length put away all sins we come to that blessed state of glory which has been obtained for us by the blood of your Son. Amen.[5]

❧ Lesson 2 ❧
Introducing Jonah

II Kings 14:23-29

Part I: Setting the Stage

Purpose
This lesson introduces us to Jonah by exploring a little-known episode that confirms Jonah's career as a successful prophet in Israel. It is important for us to realize that Jonah was a real, historical person and a respected man of God whose life and writings are to be taken seriously.

Look for the following application points in this lesson:

1. God uses unexpected methods and people to further His plans of salvation.
2. Prosperity alone cannot solve social problems because there are underlying spiritual issues.
3. We must continue to obey God's word and His call on our lives rather than coasting on our reputation of past obedience.

A Faithful Prophet
Not many people think of Jonah as a faithful prophet. In his own unflattering testimony in the book of Jonah he tells of the time he disobeyed God's command to preach in Nineveh, Assyria, by trying to flee to the far side of the Mediterranean Sea. His great escape was a disaster, of course. God stopped Jonah's flight with a storm, rescued him with a big fish, and gave him a second chance to obey. Jonah went to Nineveh but his will was still

not conformed to God's. At the end of the book we sense that God is not yet finished with Jonah.

You might be surprised to find that apart from Jonah's book, Scripture portrays Jonah as a credible, faithful prophet. We will see in Lesson 8 that Jesus refers to Jonah with respect. Jonah is the only minor prophet mentioned by Jesus,[6] and the only Old Testament figure Jesus compares Himself to. It is a curious fact that the one person in Scripture who criticizes Jonah is Jonah himself. This insight will be worth remembering as we study Jonah.

In the book of Second Kings we learn a few details about Jonah's personal background and his successful prophetic ministry in Israel. The record indicates that at some point God gave Jonah an important message to prophesy to the king of Israel. A brief but significant report of Jonah's faithful obedience is tucked away in the historical narrative concerning King Jeroboam II.

A Time of Material Wealth and Spiritual Poverty
Jonah's prophetic ministry occurred during a time of unusual prosperity in Israel. It was one of the longest periods of economic and military expansion that Israel ever experienced. Many people were living in luxury with sumptuous food and wine, ivory mansions, and summer homes. They lounged and enjoyed an idleness known only to those with abundant wealth. This was the Israel of Jonah's day; he lived in a prosperous time.

But there was another side to life in Israel during these good times. Ironically, although it was a period of great material prosperity it was also a time of great wickedness. The wealthy abused their power to oppress the poor and pervert justice in the courts. They stole even the smallest items from those who could not defend themselves. From the kings and priests on down, God's law was trampled. This too was the Israel of Jonah's day; he lived in an evil time.

God sent a number of prophets to guide Israel back to Him. Jonah prophesied the good news of Israel's deliverance from Syrian control and the restoration of Israel's borders. Hosea and Amos preached the need for repentance due to injustice and false worship. The prophets' messages were a package deal. God intended His covenant blessing of land to be met with the people's covenant obedience to His word.

A Real Prophet

Despite the account in Second Kings, today it is common for critics to dismiss Jonah as a fairy tale character suited for bedtime stories and cartoons. However, Scripture consistently affirms that Jonah was a credible historical figure whose career encompassed national and international politics. He advised one of the most successful kings that ever ruled the northern kingdom of Israel, and his preaching influenced the king of Assyria.

Outside of Scripture, Jonah is referred to as a historical person in several books of the Apocrypha, by the 1st century Jewish historian Josephus, and in other places. Scholars in the past, unlike today, have been nearly unanimous in considering the person and events in the life of Jonah to be real. The narrative in Second Kings confirms that God used His very real and obedient prophet Jonah to further His saving purposes. Jonah is someone we can take seriously.

Part II: Studying Scripture

Read II Kings 14:23-29

1. Jonah's Background

We do not have a great deal of personal information about Jonah, but we know he was a prophet during the reign of King Jeroboam II of Israel in the 8th century B.C. The idolatrous and evil Jeroboam reigned for an exceptional length of time from about 793-753 B.C., including eleven years as co-regent with his father Joash (Jehoash).

Jonah was from Gath-hepher, a moderate-size city within the tribe of Zebulun in Israel. Gath-hepher was located about twelve miles west of the Sea of Galilee and three miles northeast of Nazareth. Jewish tradition speculates among other things that Jonah was the son of the widow of Zarephath whom Elijah raised from the dead, or possibly the young prophet who anointed King Jehu. These intriguing speculations are not verified by Scripture but affirm Jonah's reputation as a noteworthy figure in the Old Testament.

a) Jeroboam II was the fourteenth king in the northern kingdom of Israel. The kings of Israel were generally wicked. In v. 24, how is Jeroboam II described?

b) Read I Kings 12:26-33. The wickedness of Jeroboam II was like Jeroboam I a century earlier. Jeroboam I was the first king in the northern kingdom of Israel.[7] What were the sins of Jeroboam I?

c) Doing evil in the eyes of the Lord has two main components: turning away from God and serving other gods. When kings or leaders repeatedly do evil in the eyes of the Lord, what happens to the nation? Why do you think the people of Israel followed their kings into idolatry and how could it have been prevented?

d) In your opinion, are people today willing to resist national leaders who turn from God? Explain your answer. How will you resist being misled by such leaders?

2. Jonah's Calling

a) In v. 25, Jonah's name in Hebrew is *Yonah ben-Amittai*, literally "Dove, son of Truth." It is tempting to find some special significance in his name. Perhaps Truth was the name of Jonah's father or a term describing Jonah's character or calling. The dove was a symbol of reconciliation with God. For example, a dove brought an olive branch to Noah after the Flood, and doves were an acceptable sacrifice for the poor. They were gentle birds. How do doves respond to storms and distress (see Psalm 55:6-8)?

b) In v. 25, Jonah is called God's servant (*ebed*). It is the same word Isaiah calls God's Suffering Servant, the Messiah. What does the concept of being God's servant indicate about how Jonah is supposed to carry out his ministry?

c) In v. 25, Jonah is also called God's prophet or spokesperson (*navi*, "called one"). True prophets were not chosen by any human being. What are the implications of being God's called one with regard to Jonah's preaching? To whom is Jonah accountable?

3. Jonah's Message

Jonah must have had mixed feelings about predicting military victory for Jeroboam II. On one hand, Jeroboam was an undeniably wicked king. On the other hand, God's people were in need of deliverance from Syria and God had chosen the timing and the means by which to save them. The Bible does not say whether Jonah resented this assignment or rejoiced in it. It simply records his obedience and God's fulfillment of the prophecy.

a) Syria (Aram) was a problem for Israel in Jonah's day. In v. 26, what phrases indicate Israel was being oppressed? What allies could Israel count on for help?

b) In v. 27, what phrase indicates that the oppression was serious and Israel was in danger of being crushed by Syria unless God intervened?

c) The timing for restoring Israel's border with Syria was providential. Syria was distracted by military attacks from its neighbor Assyria, a historic enemy of Syria and Israel. Although Assyria was in a temporary period of stagnation due to internal rebellions and aggression by Urartu (Armenia), Assyria's attacks had weakened Syria, providing a window of opportunity for Israel. In v. 27, God chose wicked Jeroboam II to be

His instrument of salvation for Israel. What does this tell you about God's methods for accomplishing His saving purposes?

d) In v. 28, it was a major accomplishment for Jeroboam to restore Israel's northern border with Syria, including control of the cities of Damascus and Lebo-hamath which Israel had controlled under David and Solomon. Jeroboam continued to expand the border east of the Jordan River into Ammon and Moab as far south as the Dead Sea (Sea of the Arabah). Why would Jeroboam trust Jonah's prophecy enough to take military action?

e) Following Jeroboam's death there was an ongoing struggle for power in Israel. A series of six kings ruled without prophetic sanction, weakening the nation. Who do you think Israel was really rejecting when it refused to consult God's prophets about choosing a king? (See Hosea 8:1-4)

Read Hosea 4:1-2, 17; 5:1, 14

4. Jonah's Contemporary: Hosea

Hosea was also a prophet in Israel during Jeroboam's reign, but we do not know if Hosea knew Jonah. Hosea's negative message to Israel was certainly different from Jonah's positive one. God told Hosea to act out his message by marrying the prostitute Gomer who represented Israel, God's beloved but unfaithful bride. Hosea broadens our understanding of what was going on in Israel.

a) What were the charges Hosea brought against Israel?

4:1-2 _____

4:17 _____

b)   In 5:1, who did Hosea blame for Israel's wickedness?

c)   In 5:14, what would be God's judgment against Israel?

Read Amos 2:6-8, 12; 3:11; 4:1-3; 6:4-6

5. Jonah's Contemporary: Amos

Amos was another prophet in Israel during Jeroboam's reign, but we do not know if he knew Hosea and Jonah. Like Hosea, Amos spoke harsh judgment against Israel.

a)   What were the charges Amos brought against Israel? Consider these in addition to Hosea's charges to get a sense of the extent of injustice in Israel.

2:6-8   _____

2:12   _____

6:4-6   _____

b)   In 3:11 and 4:1-3, what would be God's judgment against Israel? Note that the Assyrians were known for brutal warfare, including leading away prisoners of war by linking them together with ropes attached to hooks in their noses or lips.

c)   When we read the prophecies of all three prophets, Jonah, Hosea, and Amos, we get a more complete picture of the situation in Israel. Economic prosperity and military expansion of Israel's borders were accompanied by widespread spiritual arrogance among the leaders and people. There was blatant disregard for the poor, increased idolatry, and all kinds of immorality. Explain in your own words why prosperity is often associated with injustice.

d) In our prosperous country today, what kinds of injustice are you aware of? Why do social problems still exist despite the extensive efforts of government programs and charitable organizations to address them? What are the underlying spiritual issues? Why is Jesus Christ the only answer?

6. The Need for Continuing Obedience

We do not know which came first, Jonah's obedience in Second Kings or God's call in the book of Jonah. Many scholars suggest that the Second Kings episode occurred first. If so, perhaps Jonah's obedience in Israel and his privileged role as a successful prophet made him feel he had earned the right to pass judgment on God's assignment to Nineveh.

Author Sinclair Ferguson warns that neither Jonah nor we should rely on our reputation for past obedience to God as an excuse to avoid present obedience:

> "*No past privilege, nor all past privileges together; no past obedience, nor fruitfulness in service, can ever substitute for present obedience to the Word of God.* Great blessings only bring present fruitfulness when they are met with continuing obedience."[8]

a) Our past obedience to God does not relieve us from obeying Him today. Name some areas where you used to do a better job of obeying God's word than you do now. What changes will you make to ensure present obedience in those areas?

b) What are some of the lessons you have learned from past obedience to God's word that can help or inspire you to continue to be obedient in the future?

Part III: Personal Application and Growth

Today's lesson points to several important truths that apply to our personal lives. Allow these truths to penetrate your mind, soften your heart, deepen your faith and affect your behavior to help you continually grow in Christ.

1. God uses unexpected methods and people to further His plans of salvation.

In your personal life what unexpected and perhaps unwelcome methods or people is God using to further His plans and develop your spiritual maturity? How will you respond to God this week when you don't like His ways, keeping in mind that God is always working out His good purposes?

2. Prosperity alone cannot solve social problems because there are underlying spiritual issues.

What practical steps will you take to address the spiritual aspect of social problems in your community? What obstacles do you anticipate? How will you remain spiritually strong when you encounter opposition to your efforts?

3. We must continue to obey God's word and His call on our lives rather than coasting on our reputation of past obedience.

What new thing do you feel God is calling you to do? How will you overcome any reluctance you have to obeying His call?

Part IV: Closing Prayer

by John Calvin

Grant, Almighty God, that as you have not sent a Jonah to us when alienated from every hope of salvation, but have given your Son to be our teacher, clearly to show to us the way of salvation, and not only to call us to repentance by threatening and terrors, but also kindly to allure us to the hope of eternal life, and to be a pledge of your paternal love;

O grant that we may not reject so remarkable a favor offered to us, but willingly and from the heart obey you;

And though the condition which you set before us in your gospel may seem hard, and though the bearing of the cross is bitter to our flesh, yet may we never shun to obey you, but present ourselves to you as a sacrifice;

And having overcome all the hindrances of this world, may we thus proceed in the course of our holy calling, until we be at length gathered into your celestial kingdom, under the guidance of Christ your Son, our Lord. Amen.[9]

❧ Lesson 3 ❦
Jonah's Disobedience
Jonah 1:1-16

Before starting this lesson, please take time to read all four chapters of the book of Jonah to get an overview. As you read, keep in mind that the narrative is designed to elicit a response from you, a response of faith in God that grows stronger as the narrative unfolds.

Part I: Setting the Stage

Purpose
Today's lesson looks at the opening verses of the book of Jonah. God told His prophet Jonah to preach in Nineveh, Assyria, but Jonah rebelled. It is important for us to realize that it is futile to try to run away from God and it is sinful to disobey His word.

Look for the following application points in this lesson:

1.   Our obedience to God should be immediate and active.
2.   We are never out of God's sight, nor can we thwart His purposes.
3.   God guides us by His written word and sometimes by circumstances, but we should never be guided by circumstances that conflict with His word.

Author of the Book of Jonah
We do not know who wrote the book of Jonah, for the book is anonymous. Since many details could only have been supplied by Jonah, this study joins the ranks of commentators who attribute authorship to the prophet Jonah.

Date

This study accepts the view that Jonah wrote his book near the end of his ministry during the reign of Jeroboam II from 793-753 B.C. This dating is consistent with the observation that Jonah does not portray Assyria as an imminent threat to Israel's existence. It was not until the sudden rise of Tiglath-Pileser III in 745 B.C. that Assyria became a global empire, setting the stage for the eventual destruction of Israel in 722 B.C.

Literary Genre

Scholars note that the book of Jonah is quite different from books of other minor prophets, for it focuses on events surrounding Jonah's mission more than his actual prophetic message. Another difference is the record of several miracles. Since critics today assume that miracles are impossible, they consider the book of Jonah to be a fictional account or extended parable. However, there are factors that argue persuasively against the critics' view.

For one thing, Scripture attests to the events in the story of Jonah as having actually happened. Jesus regards Jonah's captivity in the great fish, Jonah's preaching, and Nineveh's repentance as historical events. In addition, the story is unusually long and complex for a parable. In agreement with the majority of scholars throughout history, this study will treat the book of Jonah not as a fictional parable, but as a historical prophetic narrative.

Audience

The book of Jonah was most likely written to warn people in the northern kingdom of Israel to repent while there was still time to avoid destruction, as the people of Nineveh had done. Unfortunately, Israel remained unrepentant. As a result, God used Assyria as His vehicle of punishment against Israel.

Themes

Listed below are several important themes in the book of Jonah. This study focuses on the theme of theodicy, defined earlier as the justification or explanation of God's ways with regard to evil in light of His goodness. The theme of theodicy provides a basis for understanding the whole book, including the perplexing incidents in the last chapter.

Theodicy	*Why does a good God allow sin? (4:2)*
Missions	*God wants to be known in the whole world. (1:2; 3:1)*
Obedience	*We should obey God's call on our lives. (1:3)*
God's Sovereignty	*God does as He pleases. (1:14)*
Salvation	*Salvation comes from the Lord. (2:9)*
God's Grace	*God shows compassion, patience and love. (4:2)*
Universal Lordship	*God rules and loves the peoples of the world. (4:11)*

Outline

The following is a simple way to look at the book of Jonah:

Chapter 1	Jonah's disobedience and God's response
Chapter 2	Jonah's prayer and God's response
Chapters 3-4	Jonah's reluctant obedience and God's response

Part II: Studying Scripture

Read Jonah 1:1-3

1. God's Call

The book of Jonah opens with the customary words introducing an oracle from God to His prophets: "The word of the LORD came to…" We do not know exactly how God impressed His call on Jonah, but Jonah was certain it was God's word and he knew that God wanted him to arise, go, and call out.

a) Arise! In Hebrew when the imperative form of "arise" is coupled with another verb, it conveys urgency. In v. 2, it was not that Jonah should literally stand up from a sitting position, but that he was to obey without delay (note that some translations omit "arise.") Why does God want us to respond to His call on our lives now, not later? What does our hesitation indicate?

b) Go! God's call on our lives is not always convenient. Sometimes He requires us to go to a new place for missions, study, family, or jobs. Has God ever called you to a new place for His purposes? What was your response? What will you do to respond even better next time? Missionary Elisabeth Elliot emphasizes that our obedience to God's call must be active even if His call is not what we anticipated:

> "This is the point at which earth and heaven meet, the point at which my will must come into harmony with God's... If in the integrity of my heart I speak the words, *Thy will be done,* I must be willing, if the answer requires it, that *my* will be undone. It is a prayer of commitment and relinquishment... He calls us not to passivity but to dynamic self-abandonment that commitment to his kingdom means."[10]

c) Call out! Jonah was to preach God's prophecy of judgment against Nineveh. Jonah knew it was a conditional prophecy and it made him angry to know that if the wicked Assyrians repented, God might not punish them. Jonah wanted God to act justly and punish sin. When we demand that God's justice prevail rather than His mercy, what do we forget about our own sinful condition? How do you react when God is merciful to others?

2. Destination: Nineveh

Nineveh was possibly the greatest city in the world in Jonah's time. It was not yet the capital of the Assyrian empire, for Assyria would not become a world empire until the rise of Tiglath-Pileser III in 745 B.C., but the city boasted a royal residence and other important buildings.

a) Nineveh was a city known for violence, an insatiable appetite for power, merciless military conquest, paganism, materialism, and arrogance. What practical changes would you expect to occur if the people listened to Jonah's warning and truly repented of their sinfulness?

b) Read Nahum 1:11. A century after Jonah's ministry the prophet Nahum of Judah preached against Nineveh. By then Nineveh was the capital of the Assyrian empire, and Assyria had destroyed Israel and reduced Judah to a vassal state. Nineveh's spiritual condition was worse than before Jonah's preaching. What was Nineveh's attitude toward God?

c) Read Nahum 3:1-3. The Assyrians were known for committing unspeakable atrocities against their enemies (skinning them alive, cutting off body parts, etc.). What was Nineveh's attitude toward people? How do you suppose disdain for people and for God gets such a firm hold in a culture?

3. Fleeing from God

Nineveh was 500 miles northeast of Israel, but Jonah booked passage on a freighter headed for Tarshish, a city unknown to us. Tarshish was probably not Tarsus of Syria, for the route to Tarsus was initially the same as to Nineveh and Jonah was trying to run the other way. Tarshish was most likely the metal mining port of Tartessus in southern Spain located 1,000 miles west of Israel. Jonah's refusal to go to Nineveh was evidently not due to Nineveh's great distance if Jonah was willing to flee twice as far in the opposite direction.

a) The fare to Tarshish would have cost Jonah a great deal more than going to Nineveh. Jonah's disobedience to God was costly in terms of money. In what ways besides money is disobedience and sin costly? What has our sin cost God? (See I Peter 1:18-19; Acts 20:28)

b) Jonah tried to flee from God's presence but he would have known it was impossible to succeed. God is omniscient (all-knowing), omnipotent (all-powerful), and omnipresent (present everywhere). As the psalmist says,[11]

> "Where shall I go from your Spirit? Or where shall I flee from your presence? If I ascend to heaven, you are there! If I make my bed in Sheol, you are there! If I take the wings of the morning and dwell in the uttermost parts of the sea, even there your hand shall lead me, and your right hand shall hold me." (Psalm 139:7-10)

Perhaps Jonah hoped to make it so difficult for God to use him that God would change His mind, or perhaps Jonah hoped the situation would resolve itself while he was gone. What wrong attitude do we reveal when we try to take matters into our own hands because we do not like God's ways?

Read Jonah 1:4-6

4. Stopped By a Storm

a) God hurled a violent storm to halt Jonah's flight. The pagan sailors knew the storm was divinely sent and they called out to their gods, probably Baal in particular since he was the Canaanite god of rain, but they could not stop the storm that way. In v. 5, how else do the sailors react to the deadly storm?

b) It is not clear whether Jonah went down to the inner part of the ship to hide or merely to sleep. It is also not clear if he went down before or after the storm began. His sound sleep seems to indicate his unconcern for whether or not he perishes, in contrast to the sailors' frantic activity. In v. 6, what request from the captain does Jonah ignore? How does the captain's command echo God's command earlier in v. 2?

c) Theologian J. I. Packer says Jonah was off-track, following the path of self-will rather than the way of God. Packer advises that when we take the wrong path in life we should turn back to God and His restoring grace:

> "The wise person will take occasion from his new troubles to check his original guidance very carefully. Trouble should always be treated as a call to consider one's ways."[12]

Are you off track in some area of your life? How can you discern whether your troubles mean you are just facing difficult times or you are being defiant toward God? If you sense that God is trying to get your attention through troubles, how will you respond?

Read Jonah 1:7-16

5. God's Sovereignty

a) When the sailors realize Jonah is the one responsible for their trouble, they want to know who he is. In v. 9-10, why does Jonah's answer terrify them?

b) In v. 12, Jonah would rather perish than turn to God and obey Him. Why do you think some people are willing to acknowledge God as Creator, yet they refuse to accept His sovereign right to rule over them?

c) In v. 13-14, what evidence do you find that the sailors do not want to harm Jonah? Whom do they rightly fear? What phrase indicates that the sailors accept God's sovereignty?

d) It is ironic that the pagan sailors cry out to God for life while Jonah would rather die than call to God. What is your opinion of Jonah's rebellious attitude toward God, considering that Jonah is God's representative?

e) In v. 16, although they may not have had saving faith, what is the sailors' appropriate reaction to the demonstration of God's control over nature?

f) Centuries after Jonah, Jesus' disciples were afraid during a violent storm on the Sea of Galilee. Like the sailors on Jonah's ship, the disciples were even more afraid when the storm was calmed. They knew that only the supreme Creator God controls nature. What do you think the disciples must have realized about Jesus, just as we should? (See Mark 4:41; see also Hebrews 1:3)

6. Our Response

a) Author Sinclair Ferguson suggests it is possible that Jonah deemed his disobedience as acceptable since God provided the ship for his escape, but circumstances and feelings are never excuses for disobedience:

> "God communicates his will fundamentally and primarily *through his revealed Word*. It is a mistake to look for God's guidance in more immediate and mystical ways – through subjective impressions in our spirits, through circumstances, through 'signs'... Do not be guided by providences when you are refusing to be guided by God's Word... When we have a heart to rebel against God there will frequently be the providential means put before us to give us the opportunity. But when we are on the run from God, his providences are *wise tests*. They are never *gracious excuses*."[13]

How will you resist the temptation to rely on your feelings and rationalizations when they conflict with God's word?

b) This lesson leaves Jonah sinking to the bottom of the Mediterranean Sea. It seems incredible that he would rather die than turn to God in repentance. We have to remember, though, that we are not so unlike Jonah. At times we too have refused to repent of sin and obey God's word. It is only by God's grace that He has not given up on us. What is your response to God's patience and His provision of salvation in Christ?

Part III: Personal Application and Growth

Today's lesson points to several important truths that apply to our personal lives. Allow these truths to penetrate your mind, soften your heart, deepen your faith and affect your behavior to help you continually grow in Christ.

1. Our obedience to God should be immediate and active.

This truth can be applied to everyday situations. For instance, the Holy Spirit often brings someone to our mind unexpectedly so that we will pray for them. How will you respond the next time God calls on you this way?

2. We are never out of God's sight, nor can we thwart His purposes.

Even when you do not like what God is doing, what will you do to avoid being rebellious like Jonah and instead cooperate with God's saving purposes?

3. God guides us by His written word and sometimes by circumstances, but we should never be guided by circumstances that conflict with His word.

We are constantly presented with opportunities to do things that conflict with the teachings of the Bible. It can be easy to rationalize wrong behavior if the opportunity is there in front of us or we do not know God's teachings. What is your plan for becoming more familiar with God's word starting this week? How will you ensure that the Bible is the final authority in your life?

Part IV: Closing Prayer

by John Calvin

Grant, Almighty God, that as you set before us this day your holy prophet as an awful example of your wrath against all who are rebellious and disobedient to you;

O grant that we may learn so to subject all our thoughts and feelings to your word, that we may not reject anything that pleases you, but so learn both to live and to die for you that we may ever regard your will, and undertake nothing but what you have testified is approved by you, so that we may fight under your banners, and throughout life obey your word;

Until at length we reach that blessed rest which has been obtained for us by the blood of your only begotten Son, and is laid up for us in heaven through the hope of His gospel. Amen.[14]

❧ Lesson 4 ❦
The Grace of God

Jonah 1:17-2:10

Part I: Setting the Stage

Purpose
This lesson considers Jonah's miraculous rescue by the great fish. It is important to know that salvation is always a gracious, undeserved gift from God that should bring forth our response of gratitude and repentance.

Look for the following application points in this lesson:

1. Our laments should end in praise to God.
2. Learning the psalms and their context can be a source of strength and comfort in difficult times.
3. Repentance involves gratitude for Christ's saving work and a commitment to live obediently under His lordship.

Saved From the Depths
We left Jonah in the previous lesson sinking to the bottom of the Mediterranean Sea after being thrown overboard by the sailors in an effort to calm the storm. Jonah's situation seemed hopeless.

Imagine living in Old Testament times and hearing the story of Jonah for the first time. Listeners would surmise that Jonah had met his death in the stormy chaos of the Mediterranean Sea. God had dealt harshly but justly with His disobedient prophet. It was a sad but fitting ending to the story.

What a shock to have a miraculous fish enter the story! Modern readers are still fascinated by the sudden arrival of the fish. How could such a thing be possible? It is a bit frustrating that the Bible is not equally obsessed with the fish and does not provide more details. The story moves on as if an ordinary fishing boat picked up Jonah. The fish is treated like it is no big deal in itself, just an explanation of how God ensured that His prophet Jonah survived.

A 'Greate Fyshe'
We do not know whether the fish was a whale. The original Hebrew term *dag gadol* means "great fish." The term could possibly include whales (which are technically mammals) but since the normal usage means a huge or great fish, that is how our modern translations render it.

The popular idea that Jonah was swallowed by a whale can be traced to early translation efforts. Remember that meanings of words can evolve with time. The Hebrew phrase *dag gadol* in Jonah 1:17 and the Greek word *ketos* in Matthew 12:40, referring to the fish that swallowed Jonah, originally both meant "great fish." Over the centuries, though, the meaning of the Greek word *ketos* changed and became synonymous with "whale."

William Tyndale in 1534 therefore translated *dag gadol* as "greate fyshe" in Jonah 1:17 and *ketos* as "whale" in Matthew 12:40, apparently unaware that the meaning of the Greek word had changed over the years. Tyndale's translation became the basis for the widely accepted King James Version. Today "whale" is still found in Matthew 12:40 in the King James Version.

A Miracle
The whole fish scenario seems impossible to people who reject miracles (God's intervention into the ordinary course of nature). The idea of Jonah living in a fish is seen as a ridiculous piece of fiction, a dramatic element added by the author to embellish the story. The problem, though, is that there is not enough detail about the fish to effectively embellish anything. We do not know how big it was, where it came from, or how Jonah survived in it. Scripture does not present the fish as a dramatic literary device, but as a demonstration of God's saving grace toward Jonah.

Sometimes people do not doubt that the episode actually occurred, but they see it simply as a coincidence. They do not find anything miraculous about it. The story reminds them of similar episodes when people were accidentally swallowed by whales or sharks.[15] However, trying to rationalize the Biblical account of the fish on the basis of other episodes in history misses the point that God miraculously saved Jonah from certain death, whether by creating a special fish for the occasion or bringing an existing one along at the right time.

It was no coincidence that Jonah was rescued. We worship a God who would rather forgive and save His people than punish them. The ultimate evidence of God's saving purposes is found in the work of Jesus Christ.

Part II: Studying Scripture

Read Jonah 1:17

1. A Fish Like a Hospital

a) We should understand that the fish was a vehicle of salvation much like Noah's ark, not a vehicle of punishment. God sent the fish to rescue Jonah's life. The Reformer John Calvin makes a helpful analogy:

> "[Jonah was] received into the inside of the fish as though it were into a hospital."[16]

Nevertheless, the incident could not have been a pleasant experience for Jonah who probably remained conscious during his ordeal. Imagine and describe in your own words the sensory aspects of being in the belly of the fish (sight, sound, smell, taste, touch).

b) The mysterious fish is mentioned in only three verses in the book of Jonah (1:17; 2:1; 2:10). What do we learn about the fish in v. 17?

c) The underlying purpose of miracles is God's authentication of a message or messenger. The provision of a miraculous fish verified

Jonah's calling by God. Why do you think we do not get more details about the fish?

d) Jonah was inside the fish for "three days and three nights." This common phrase includes two nights and any part of the first and third days. It may also be an idiom for the journey between Sheol (the place of the dead) and the land of the living. If you were in Jonah's place, what would you be thinking about while you were in the fish?

Read Jonah 2:1-9

2. Rescued from Certain Death

Jonah understood that he deserved death for his disobedience to God. However, when he had the sailors throw him into the sea and he faced the actual possibility of death, he no longer wanted to run from God. In the hopelessness of his situation he cried out to his merciful God to save him.

a) Jonah prays to God from the belly of the fish that saved his life. He recalls crying to God earlier from the belly of Sheol, the place of the dead (meaning here the depths of the sea). In v. 2, what happened when Jonah cried out in the sea? When you cry out to God and He responds with saving circumstances, how quick are you to acknowledge His role?

b) In v. 3-4, who does Jonah understand hurled him into the sea? What is ironic about Jonah's lament that drowning separates him from God's presence, considering what Jonah has been trying to do up to this point?

c) In v. 5, what indicates that Jonah nearly drowned? In v. 7, how does Jonah acknowledge that he had to face the threat of death before calling out to God?

3. Giving Thanks

Jonah's prayer of thanksgiving contains echoes from about ten different psalms. Jonah especially draws on Psalm 42 as indicated below.

A Prayer of Thanksgiving

Psalm 42:7, 11	Jonah 2:3-4, 9
"Deep calls to deep	"For you cast me into the deep,
at the roar of your waterfalls;	into the heart of the seas...
all your breakers and your waves	all your waves and your billows
have gone over me...	passed over me...
"Why are you cast down, O my soul,	"I am driven away from your
and why are you in turmoil within me?	sight; yet I shall again look
Hope in God, for I shall again	upon your holy temple... I with
praise him,	the voice of thanksgiving
my salvation and my God."	will sacrifice to you...
	Salvation belongs to the LORD!"

Psalms 42-43 together form a lament praising God in the midst of great adversity. The lament may be a description of David's attempt to hide from Saul. He flees to Mount Hermon, the source of the Jordan River where turbulent waterfalls threaten his life and sound like the "deep," the stormy Mediterranean Sea. He longs to be in God's presence and worship Him again. The psalmist, like Jonah later, knows that only God can save.

a) What can we learn from Jonah about the benefits of memorizing Scripture passages and context to recall in difficult times? What efforts have you made to learn some of the psalms?

b) In v. 8, Jonah acknowledges that the attribute that distinguishes God from false gods is God's steadfast love (*hesed*). In v. 9, how does Jonah plan to honor God, just as the pagan sailors did in 1:16 when God spared them? Here we get a brief glimpse of the faithful side of Jonah.

c) Many people can identify with Jonah's prayer or psalm of lament because they have experienced the loneliness of exile due to unrealized expectations or broken relationships. What is your experience with exile or estrangement? How has God given you help and comfort when you turned to Him?

d) The dominant mood of a lament is sadness, but the final note is usually upbeat. In v. 9, how does Jonah end his lament? How will you ensure that your laments end in the same positive tone?

4. Down, Down, Down and Up

Jonah's disobedience leads him downward both physically and spiritually. When Jonah finally hits bottom God rescues him and lifts him upward.

a) In Jonah's flight away from God he physically descends from the mountains of Samaria to their hidden base. What three places represent Jonah's downward journey in the verses below? Note that in Hebrew the repetition of a term three times is like underlining or bold print.[17]

1:3 _____

1:5 _____

2:6 _____

b) Think of a time when you hit bottom because you were trying to handle a tough situation on your own and you simply ran out of strength and ideas, or you had a problem that could not be solved. Why does it sometimes take us so long to turn to God for help? What will you do to turn to Him sooner?

c) In 2:6, what is the only hope of salvation for Jonah? For us?

Read Jonah 2:10

5. Vomited Out

References to the fish in 1:17 and 2:10 form an *inclusio* or enclosure around Jonah's prayer, a common Hebrew technique for including poetry in a prose narrative in a way that makes the poem stand out.

a) Why does the fish release Jonah? What does this tell us about God's word?

b) Look up the definition of the unpleasant word "vomited." Vomit is used elsewhere in the Bible in connection with disobedience to God's word.[18] For example, how were the Israelites to be cursed if they disobeyed God's covenant commands? (See Leviticus 18:26-28)

c) What will Jesus spit out (literally, "vomit") at the end times because it failed to produce good works as God commanded? (See Revelation 3:15-16)

d) When the fish vomits Jonah out in response to God's command, we get the impression God is not entirely pleased with Jonah. While it is true that Jonah is sincerely thankful for salvation, his heart is evidently not yet in line with God's word. Why is it significant that Jonah's prayer fails to mention sin, guilt, shame, remorse, repentance, or a desire for forgiveness?

6. Our Lord and Savior

Jonah's thanksgiving prayer is sometimes called his prayer of repentance, but at best it is more like a prayer of partial repentance. Elements of true repentance are missing such as heartfelt sorrow for sin, confession of sin, yearning for forgiveness, and a commitment to live a new life in accordance with God's will. In the next lesson when Jonah finally obeys God's command to go to Nineveh, he seems motivated more by a desire to avoid further punishment than a desire to please God. Jonah gratefully accepts God as his Savior but does not allow God to be his Lord.

The Old Testament teaches that God is both Lord and Savior. He is willing to save His people, but they must turn to Him and submit to His ways:

> "Who told this long ago? Who declared it of old? Was it not I, the LORD? And there is no other god besides me, a righteous God and a Savior; there is none besides me. Turn to me and be saved, all the ends of the earth!" (Isaiah 45:21-22)

Similarly, the New Testament teaches that Jesus is both Lord and Savior:

> "For unto you is born this day in the city of David a Savior, who is Christ the Lord." (Luke 2:11)

We cannot truly worship Christ as one without the other, because when we turn toward Christ for salvation we have to simultaneously turn away from our sins. Turning to Christ means letting Him reign in our lives as Lord.[19]

a) What does it look like in your everyday life for Christ to be both your Lord and Savior?

39

b) How will you counsel someone who wants the benefits of salvation but is not willing to submit to Christ as Lord?

Part III: Personal Application and Growth

Today's lesson points to several important truths that apply to our personal lives. Allow these truths to penetrate your mind, soften your heart, deepen your faith and affect your behavior to help you continually grow in Christ.

1. Our laments should end in praise to God.

Write a brief heartfelt prayer to God about something that is currently troubling you, ending with confidence and praise for who God is and the saving works He has done in the past. Pray this lament several times this week to develop the habit of taking your concerns to God with praise.

2. Learning the psalms and their context can be a source of strength and comfort in difficult times.

Jonah drew comfort and strength from psalms he had memorized. This week memorize part of a psalm to recall in times of distress. Perhaps start with a verse from the psalm in today's lesson:

> "Why are you cast down, O my soul, and why are you in turmoil within me? Hope in God; for I shall again praise him, my salvation and my God." (Psalm 42:11)

3. Repentance involves gratitude for Christ's saving work and a commitment to live obediently under His lordship.

Identify one area in your life where you are reluctant to let Jesus Christ be your Lord. What step will you take to repent and submit your will to His authority in this area? What positive results do you hope to experience?

Part IV: Closing Prayer

by John Calvin

Grant, Almighty God, that as you had once given us such an evidence of your infinite power in your servant Jonah, whose mind, when he was almost sunk down into Sheol, you had yet raised up to yourself, and had so supported with firm constancy that he ceased not to pray and to call on you;

O grant that in the trials by which we must be daily exercised, we may raise upwards our minds to you and never cease to think that you are near us;

And that when the signs of your wrath appear, and when our sins thrust themselves before our eyes to drive us to despair, may we still constantly struggle and never surrender the hope of your mercy;

Until having finished all our contests, we may at length freely and fully give thanks to you, and praise your infinite goodness such as we daily experience, that being conducted through continual trials, we may at last come into that blessed rest which is laid up for us in heaven, through Christ our Lord. Amen.[20]

❧ Lesson 5 ❧
Jonah's Evangelism
Jonah 3:1-10

Part I: Setting the Stage

Purpose

Today's lesson looks at Jonah's evangelistic efforts and Nineveh's repentance. It is important to remember that although conversion is the work of the Holy Spirit, He uses all kinds of people as His instruments to spread the gospel.

Look for the following application points in this lesson:

1. There are about seven billion people in the world and every single one of them is important to God no matter where they live.
2. God wants to use your personal testimony and abilities for evangelism purposes.
3. We are forgiven in Christ and so in gratitude we are to forgive others.

A City Prepared By God

Jonah traveled to Nineveh soon after his rescue by the great fish. The results of Jonah's preaching in Nineveh would turn any evangelist green with envy. Widespread repentance in response to God's message was so immediate that many critics consider it proof that the book of Jonah is fictional. Is such a miraculous revival possible?

The answer is yes, such a revival is possible. Scholars suggest that a series of ominous events had set the Assyrians on edge prior to Jonah's arrival. These events were considered divine omens of impending doom for the king and country. Through these signs or perhaps simply by the Holy Spirit, God prepared the hearts of the Ninevites to accept Jonah's message. The following signs occurred during the Assyrian reigns of Shalmaneser IV (783-774 B.C.) and his brother Assur-dan III (773-756 B.C.), about the same time Jeroboam II ruled Israel (793-753 B.C.):[21]

- Total solar eclipse in 763 B.C., an especially ominous sign.
- Intermittent famine and plague from 765-759 B.C.
- Riots against the king in various cities due to the famine.
- Enemy invasions by Urartu (Armenia) in the north.
- An earthquake, perhaps during the reign of Assur-dan III.

With God's preparation, by the time Jonah showed up in Nineveh with a message of divine judgment even the king was ready to do whatever it took to avoid disaster. Perhaps Jonah's tale of miraculous rescue along with his odd appearance due to bleaching from piscine gastric juices caught people's attention. The whole city listened to the strange foreign prophet who had traveled five hundred miles to deliver his God's word to them.

Repentance

The Ninevites repented outwardly, giving up their violent ways upon hearing Jonah's preaching. It is not certain if their repentance was evidence of saving faith since there is no indication they gave up their other gods, but their changed behavior pleased God, evoked His mercy, and averted punishment.

True repentance that accompanies saving faith consists not only of outward behavioral changes but inner heartfelt sorrow for past sin, a resolve to forsake sin in the future, and a commitment to live in obedience to God. See Psalm 51 for an example of King David's true repentance.

Revival by the Holy Spirit

Religious revival can spread like wildfire by the power of the Holy Spirit. For example, the Welsh awakening of 1859 spread to Coleraine, Northern Ireland, on June 6 with the testimony of a young schoolboy that he had the Lord Jesus in his heart. Classmates prayed with him, then teachers, parents, clergy, and townspeople joined in. Within twenty-four hours thousands in the town had been converted, and by the next day thousands more.[22]

The later Welsh revival in 1904-05 affected all aspects of life. Rough coal miners started the workday with prayer, sang hymns in the coal shafts, and cursed so little that pit ponies couldn't understand the confusing new language. Chapels became the center of cultural activity involving large numbers for choral singing. Attendance at theaters and sports events decreased and many pubs, police stations and courthouses had to close for loss of business.

The responsibility for conversion and revival belongs to the Holy Spirit who regenerates people's hearts and gives them faith. Our job is to be the Spirit's willing instruments, boldly and kindly proclaiming God's word and showing the love of Christ to a hurting world through our actions and words. God will ultimately accomplish His purposes whether or not we take part in evangelism, but we have the privilege of glorifying Him when we are obedient to His command to take the gospel of Jesus Christ to the world.

Part II: Studying Scripture

Read Jonah 3:1-5

1. A Second Chance

a) The second half of the book of Jonah begins with the same three verbs God spoke in 1:2 commanding Jonah to "arise," "go," and "call out." Again there is a sense of urgency with the word "arise" (omitted in some translations). God gives Jonah a second chance to obey. In v. 3, what is Jonah's response?

b) Read John 21:15-19. We worship a God who wants to give people a second chance. After the apostle Peter denied knowing Jesus three times during His arrest, how did the resurrected Jesus give Peter a second chance?

c) Sometimes we cannot make amends with the people we have hurt through our past disobedience. However, we can try not to repeat the same errors with others. What is an area in your life where you have made mistakes but God has given you a fresh start elsewhere? How will you avoid making the same mistakes you have made in the past?

d) We cannot relive our childhood, but if yours was unpleasant allow Christ to redeem it. He can transform hurtful things from the past so they yield something positive. In a sense, we get a second chance at a happy childhood by providing one for someone else. What have you learned from your past that will help you create or contribute to a wholesome life for a child today?

2. Important to God

In v. 3, the original Hebrew says Nineveh was a great city "to God" (*le Elohim*). Our translations treat the phrase *le Elohim* here as a superlative meaning "exceedingly" or "very," but elsewhere in the Bible the phrase consistently means "to God." The pagan city of Nineveh was not just large and important in worldly terms, but important to God.

a) Archaeological excavations of ancient Nineveh in modern Iraq began in the 19th century. Among other things, grand palaces, gardens, extensive libraries, and fine works of art were discovered. Modern cities boast similar features. What is it that makes a city important in the world's eyes?

b) What do you think it means that Nineveh was a great city in God's eyes?

3. Evangelism in the City

In v. 3, the original Hebrew says Nineveh was a "three days journey." Translators offer a number of interpretations. Some think it took three days to walk the breadth of the city. However, in Jonah's time the city wall was 3 miles in circumference with a 1-mile diameter; the suburbs of greater Nineveh later spread out to a circumference of 60 miles with a 19-mile diameter.[23] Either way it would not have taken three days to walk straight across the city.

Others think the phrase reflects ancient near-eastern etiquette. A stranger would arrive the first day and introduce himself to local leaders, preach the second day, and bid farewell the third day. Thus a visit would require three days. According to this view the phrase implies that the city was large enough for such protocol to be appropriate.

a) God cares about all the people of the world including the masses living in big cities. About half the people in the world now live in urban areas and the percentage is much higher in the United States. What are some challenges of evangelizing in urban areas in general and foreign cities in particular?

b) Read Acts 17:1-3, 17. On his second missionary journey the apostle Paul made it a point to evangelize in the provincial capital cities of Thessalonica, Corinth, and Ephesus, as well as the important city of Athens. What was his custom upon arriving in a new city? Why do you suppose Paul headed for large capital cities?

c) Read Revelation 21:23-25. Heaven is described in terms of a beautiful city on earth, the future New Jerusalem. The unity of God's people in the New Jerusalem is symbolized by the twelve tribes of Israel representing Old Testament believers, together with the twelve apostles representing New Testament believers, including us. What do you find encouraging about the description of heaven as a place with no night, a place where everyone will walk in the light of God's glory?

4. Jonah's Message

God used Jonah's preaching to warn the people of Nineveh. With regard to Jonah's actual message, commentators are divided as to whether v. 4 is the whole message or a summary. It is likely there was more to Jonah's preaching than just one sentence. For instance, people somehow learned that the message was from Jonah's God.

a) Jonah preached that Nineveh would be overthrown in forty days. This was a conditional prophecy. Read Jeremiah 18:7-10, the classic teaching about fulfillment of prophetic warnings in light of contingencies (possibilities). What does God want as a result of His warnings?

b) "Forty days" is an expression that indicates there is still some time left but judgment is coming soon. Why do people today assume they can indefinitely put off thinking about salvation and giving their lives to Christ? What is wrong with that kind of thinking? What will you do to encourage a loved one not to procrastinate any longer about taking Jesus Christ seriously?

c) In v. 5, the Ninevites rightly believed Jonah's message was from God. What was their immediate response to the threat of judgment?

d) Jonah was told by God what to preach in a specific situation and we should not imitate his pronouncement of judgment. Our job is to offer words of hope and comfort to a hurting world, assuring them that those who repent and put their trust in Jesus Christ are saved from God's judgment and wrath. Evangelism should always be grounded in love even though evangelistic methods may vary. What is your experience with effective evangelism either as someone being evangelized or the one evangelizing? What will you do to allow God to make you more effective?

e) During the Great Awakening in 1741 the Puritan theologian Jonathan Edwards delivered perhaps the most famous sermon in American history, "Sinners in the Hands of an Angry God." Edwards pictured a spider dangling over a flame, representing the precarious spiritual position of those who live without Christ. He quietly warned that for unrepentant sinners "the day of their calamity is at hand" (Deuteronomy 32:35). Then he pictured Christ flinging the door of mercy wide open, inviting poor sinners to enter. He described those who come to Christ:

> "[They are living] now in a happy state, with their hearts filled with love to Him who has loved them and washed them from their sins in His own blood, and rejoicing in hope of the glory of God."[24]

His congregation was deeply convicted of their need for salvation in Christ. It was not the messenger but the message applied by the Holy Spirit that touched their hearts. If you are timid about evangelizing, how does it give you confidence to know that the gospel is powerful even if you are not?

f) In what way does it encourage you to realize that God can use all kinds of personalities and faith testimonies, including yours, to achieve His goals?

Read Jonah 3:6-10

5. Who Knows?

a) In v. 6, how did the king respond to Jonah's message?

b) In v. 7-8, the king also responded by issuing a decree. Assyrian kings at this point in history were somewhat weak. A joint decree between the king and his nobles was unusual and perhaps implies the king needed their consent. It was not customary at that time to include animals in the decree, either, but the king was desperate. Briefly summarize each of the main requirements of the king's decree.

c) In v. 9-10, what result did the king hope for and what happened?

6. God's Forgiveness

a) Jews today read the book of Jonah every year in the afternoon of Yom Kippur, the annual Day of Atonement, because the book emphasizes God's willingness to forgive those who repent. How does the story of God's compassion in the Old Testament book of Jonah prepare us for the good news of Jesus Christ in the New Testament?

b) We worship a God who is justified in punishing sin and yet delights in showing compassion. How has God shown compassion to you?

c) What are some ways you will extend compassion and forgiveness to others who have offended you, while not allowing them to continue to harm you?

Part III: Personal Application and Growth

Today's lesson points to several important truths that apply to our personal lives. Allow these truths to penetrate your mind, soften your heart, deepen your faith and affect your behavior to help you continually grow in Christ.

1. There are about seven billion people in the world and every single one of them is important to God no matter where they live.

How will this truth change the way you think and feel about people who live in different places and circumstances from you? What large city in the world will you pray for today, lifting up believers and unbelievers alike to the Lord?

2. God wants to use your personal testimony and abilities for evangelism purposes.

What are the most compelling aspects of your personal story of coming to faith? With whom will you share your story this week to awaken a longing in them to know more of Jesus Christ? How will your faith grow as a result of sharing your testimony?

3. We are forgiven in Christ and so in gratitude we are to forgive others.

It can be hard to forgive major offenses against us, but it is also hard to forgive lesser offenses. Starting today, what change will you make in the way you react to minor slights? How do you think practicing everyday forgiveness will improve your relationships? How will the habit of everyday forgiveness prepare you to face more complicated issues of forgiveness?

Part IV: Closing Prayer

by John Calvin

Grant, Almighty God, that as there is so much timidity in us that none of us is prepared to follow where you may call us, we may be so instructed by the example of your servant Jonah as to obey you in everything;

And that though Satan and the world may oppose us with all their terrors, we may yet be strengthened by a reliance on your power and protection which you have promised to us, and may go on in the course of our calling and never turn aside, but thus contend against all the hindrances of this world until we reach that celestial kingdom where we shall enjoy you and Christ, your only begotten Son, who is our strength and our salvation;

And may your Spirit quicken us and strengthen all our faculties that we may obey you, and that at length your name may be glorified in us, and that we may finally become partakers of that glory to which you invite us through Christ our Lord. Amen.[25]

❧ Lesson 6 ❧
Jonah's Cranky Prayer
Jonah 4:1-5

Part I: Setting the Stage

Purpose

This lesson finds Jonah frustrated and cranky when God extends mercy to wicked Nineveh. Jonah knows it is God's nature to relent from sending disaster, but Jonah would rather see wickedness punished. It is important for us to accept the truth that the attributes of mercy and justice exist perfectly in God. We should never put ourselves in a position to judge His character and actions as wrong.

Look for the following application points in this lesson:

1. God is gracious, merciful, slow to anger, abounding in love, and relenting from disaster.
2. We should praise God for generously providing unearned blessings to us.
3. Christians are to be excellent goers or senders with a heart for missions.

Descriptions of God

Think about what you would say if someone asked you what God is like. Would you describe God in terms of His character, actions, or existential nature? Some people explain God in terms of what He is not, such as uncreated and unlimited. It is a daunting task to find words that capture the essential nature of an infinite God who is beyond description.

Jesus told the Samaritan woman, "God is spirit" (John 4:24). The apostle John said, "God is light" (I John 1:5) and "God is love" (I John 4:16). The prophet Jonah recites a classic Old Testament formulation that is worth memorizing. It is a condensed version of God's self-revelation in Exodus 34:6. Jonah lists five characteristics of God:

> "I knew that you are a gracious God and merciful, slow to anger and abounding in steadfast love, and relenting from disaster." (Jonah 4:2)

The 17th century Westminster Shorter Catechism offers another description of God that is worth memorizing:

> "God is a Spirit, infinite, eternal, and unchangeable, in His being, wisdom, power, holiness, justice, goodness, and truth."[26]

God's Attributes

God has attributes or characteristics not unlike people have characteristics, which is why He is called a personal or person-like God as opposed to an impersonal God. When theologians consider the many attributes of God they group them into categories to make studying them more manageable. This takes us into the realm of systematic theology.[27]

One traditional systematic approach classifies God's attributes into two major groups. Attributes that God shares to some extent with humans are called communicable attributes (i.e., love, grace, mercy, truth, justice, wisdom, holiness, goodness, and so on). We can appreciate, for instance, that people are able to love, although not in the perfect way that God loves. Attributes that belong only to God are called incommunicable attributes (i.e., self-existence, unchangeableness, perfection, eternality, omnipresence, omniscience, omnipotence, and more).

In reality God's attributes are interrelated, not separate things. God's wisdom is true, His goodness is eternal, His love is powerful. The attributes are all fused together in God's character. God will not do anything to violate His character, for He can act only in accordance with His character and nature.

Justice and Mercy

Sometimes it seems to us that God is inconsistent. There are times when God demonstrates mercy in a situation we think clearly calls for judgment. This is a major theme in the book of Jonah. Jonah could not find a reasonable theodicy (a justification or explanation of God's ways with regard to evil in light of His goodness). God's mercy to the wicked Ninevites made Jonah angry.

We have to be careful not to think we can figure God out completely. We will never be in a position where we can judge God for His actions, because we are finite creatures who cannot know everything there is to know. When we do not understand God's mysterious ways, we have to trust that God will always work in our lives for our good and for His glory, in accordance with His perfect character as revealed to us in Jesus Christ.

Part II: Studying Scripture

Read Jonah 4:1-5

1. Jonah's Anger

a) God responds to Nineveh's repentance by turning away from anger, but Jonah responds by becoming angry. In v. 1, the original Hebrew literally says God's relenting was "exceedingly evil to Jonah." What is your reaction to hearing that God's prophet arrogantly judges God's actions to be evil? How will you guard against making similar judgments against God?

b) Jonah approaches God with an angry and judgmental frame of mind. His cranky prayer begins literally, "O Lord, is this not my word…?" Jonah is more interested in his own word than God's word. Jonah seems annoyed that God has not seen the correctness of his opinion. When we demand that God see things our way and agree with us, how do we deprive ourselves of God's guidance, wisdom and fellowship?

c) Some commentators attribute Jonah's anger to intense nationalism, speculating that Jonah resented being sent to save Israel's enemy Assyria. Others suggest Jonah's anger was caused by ethnocentrism and jealousy over God's concern for Gentiles (non-Jews).[28] Perhaps it is best to rely on what Jonah himself says. In v. 2, what reason does Jonah give for his anger?

d) Jonah's understanding of God's character is based on God's self-revelation (Exodus 34:6). In your own words, contrast Jonah's character with God's:

God's Character (4:2)   Jonah's Character

Gracious   _____

Merciful and compassionate   _____

Slow to anger   _____

Abounding in steadfast love   _____

Relents from sending disaster   _____

e) If there were a column for your own character in the previous question, how would you contrast yourself to Jonah and to God? What will you do to allow God to shape your character so that it more nearly reflects His?

f) Jonah refuses to conform his will to God's. He knows God is merciful, but Jonah would rather see wickedness punished, not forgiven. He wants to see God's justice triumph over evil and he is angry that God withholds disaster from those who deserve His wrath. Why does Jonah, like us, have trouble finding the right balance between justice and mercy? What does Jonah overlook about the importance of repentance with regard to God's justice and mercy?

g) In v. 3, what does Jonah prefer to do rather than yield to God? How is this consistent with his attitude on the ship in chapter 1? What does this tell you about the incompleteness of his repentance in chapter 2?

h) People often become angry when they refuse to align their will with God's. What does our anger imply about who we think is right, us or God?

2. God's Sovereignty

a) Jonah's cranky prayer about God's grace to the Ninevites provides sharp contrast to his positive prayer about God's grace to him as he was sinking. God challenges Jonah by asking if he has any right to be angry about Nineveh. God is asking if Jonah's anger has merit and if Jonah is entitled to judge God's actions. In v. 4, what is the expected answer to God's question? Why?

b) God wants us to bring our concerns and complaints to him in prayer. However, Jonah is not asking honest questions like we see in the psalms. He is not venting his anger and then reaching a point of submission and worship. Jonah has judged God's decisions to be wrong and would prefer to die rather than see things God's way. This is incredible arrogance from a holy man of God. How will you avoid Jonah's error and cultivate a truly humble heart toward God, a heart in line with His purposes?

c) God does not owe us explanations. What did God tell Moses about His sovereignty in showing grace and mercy? (See Exodus 33:19)

3. Jonah's Continuing Defiance

a) In v. 5, Jonah is still stubbornly determined to have his way. He answers God's question about his anger with defiant action instead of words. Why does Jonah sit outside the city? What do you think he expects to happen?

b) Jonah evidently thinks the Ninevites should be destroyed and that God will soon come to the same conclusion. Perhaps Jonah hopes God will rain down burning sulfur as He did at Sodom and Gomorrah (Genesis 19:24-25). Why does Jonah, like us at times, refuse to rejoice in God's merciful ways to others? What should our attitude be?

Read Luke 15:11-32

4. Parable of the Prodigal Son

Jesus' Parable of the Prodigal Son fits Jonah's situation. The elder brother in the parable bitterly resented his father's grace toward the spendthrift younger brother. The elder brother wanted to see his brother punished and he was angry at the father's forgiveness of the repentant younger brother.

a) Based on v. 13 and 21, in what ways are the Ninevites like the younger brother in the parable?

b) Based on v. 28-30, how is Jonah like the elder brother in the parable?

c) Pastor Timothy Keller remarks that we display signs of an "elder-brother" spirit if we become not just sorrowful but angry and bitter when life does not go the way we want.[29] In v. 31-32, what is the perspective of the father, who represents God? How will you learn to see situations in your life from God's gracious point of view rather than that of the elder brother in the parable?

Read Matthew 20:1-16

5. Parable of the Vineyard Laborers

Jesus' Parable of the Vineyard Laborers can remind us of Jonah in some respects. Workers in the parable were hired at different times of the day but were paid the same amount regardless of how long they worked that day. Those who toiled longer hours resented the landowner's generosity toward latecomers who did not deserve a full day's pay.

a) The landowner, who represents God, says several important things about himself. Based on v. 13-15, how would you describe God's character?

b) The worker hired early in the day resents the landlord's generosity to the others because the others do not deserve it. Similarly, Jonah resents God's generous mercy to the Ninevites because they do not deserve it. What does this tell us about God's generosity? About God's sovereignty?

c) Most of us tend to identify with the parable's self-righteous worker hired early in the day and we resent God's generosity to undeserving people. We forget that no matter how early in life we came to faith in Jesus Christ, our salvation was an unearned gift from God. We all belong to the undeserving group. What are some unearned blessings God has generously given you? How will you avoid taking His blessings for granted?

6. Our Defiance

It is easy to criticize Jonah for his reluctance to take God's word to Nineveh. Unfortunately, most Christians are not much different than Jonah. We have too often been reluctant to obey God's command to take the gospel to the world in obedience to the Great Commission (Matthew 28:18-20). Missions is not optional. Author John Piper points out that each of us is to be either an excellent goer or an excellent sender with a global perspective:

> "Not every Christian is called to be a missionary, but every follower of Christ is called to be a world Christian. A world Christian is someone who is so gripped by the glory of God and the glory of His global purpose that he chooses to align himself with God's mission to fill the earth with the knowledge of His glory as the waters cover the sea."[30]

a)   How have you been an excellent goer or sender for foreign missions?

b)   How have you also been radical about the salvation of people in your local community?

c)   Jesus said,

> "I have other sheep that are not of this fold. I must bring them also, and they will listen to my voice. So there will be one flock, one shepherd." (John 10:16)

We should develop a heart for missions not merely as a duty or out of compassion for humanity, but first of all out of love for Christ and a desire to honor His glory and the unity of His church. How does a loving relationship with Jesus Christ affect our motivation, desire, and energy for missions?

d) Take a moment to reflect on the implications of the psalmist's words:

> "Let all the peoples praise you! Let the nations be glad and sing for joy, for you judge the peoples with equity and guide the nations upon earth." (Psalm 67:3-4)

What do you think would be the biggest changes in the world if all the nations praised God? What steps will you take to include the nations in your prayers?

Part III: Personal Application and Growth

Today's lesson points to several important truths that apply to our personal lives. Allow these truths to penetrate your mind, soften your heart, deepen your faith and affect your behavior to help you continually grow in Christ.

1. God is gracious, merciful, slow to anger, abounding in love, and relenting from disaster.

Since God has been gracious and compassionate about our many failures to live according to His word, how will you likewise extend grace and compassion to a difficult person in your life this week?

2. We should praise God for generously providing unearned blessings to us.

Some people keep an ongoing journal itemizing hundreds of undeserved blessings from God. What practical thing will you do to develop a daily attitude of gratitude? What personal growth do you hope to experience as a result of praising and thanking God through Christ more fully each day?

3. Christians are to be excellent goers or senders with a heart for missions.

People can participate in foreign and local missions through financial support, prayer, short-term trips, evangelism, mercy ministry, hospitality to missionaries, and more. In what concrete way will you expand your involvement in missions? How do you think your participation will develop your heart for missions and vice-versa?

Part IV: Closing Prayer

by John Calvin

Grant, Almighty God, that as you see us implicated in so many errors that we often fall through want of thought, and as you also see that the violent emotions of our flesh wholly blind whatever reason and judgment there is in us;

O grant that we may learn to give up ourselves altogether to obey you and so honor your wisdom as never to contend with you, though all things may happen contrary to our wishes, but patiently to wait for such an outcome as it may please you to grant;

And may we never be disturbed by any of the hindrances which Satan may throw in our way, but ever go on towards the mark which you have set before us, and never turn aside from you until, having gone through all dangers and overcome all impediments, we shall at length reach that blessed rest which has been obtained for us by the blood of your Son. Amen.[31]

❧ Lesson 7 ❧
The Sovereignty of God
Jonah 4:6-11

Part I: Setting the Stage

Purpose

This lesson brings us to the end of the book of Jonah where Jonah remains angry with his sovereign and merciful God. It is important for us to realize that Jonah's account of his sinful, arrogant disobedience teaches us to reject such foolishness and turn to our sovereign God in humility, obedience and praise. We are not to imitate Jonah's wrong example.

Look for the following application points in this lesson:

1. We need to align our will with God's, particularly in the areas of obedience to His word, mercy to others, and submission to His sovereignty.
2. Choose life by loving God, obeying His word, and holding fast to Him.
3. Lift your eyes to the bigger picture and learn to see the world from God's point of view.

God Loves the World
The book of Jonah closes with one more conversation between the cranky prophet and God. Jonah's attitude is not yet what it should be, but God does not give up on him. God asks Jonah to see things from His perspective, "And should not I pity Nineveh, that great city...?"

We all know the correct answer to God's question is that He should indeed be concerned about the great city of Nineveh. God is the Lord of the whole world. New Testament believers have the privilege of knowing that "God so loved the world, that he gave his only Son, that whoever believes in him should not perish but have eternal life." (John 3:16)

In one sense the ending of Jonah's book is extremely satisfying. God has been patient with His prophet Jonah and the people of Nineveh, and has given both of them opportunities to repent. He has exhibited His sovereign right to do as He wishes by withholding destruction and offering mercy. God has consistently acted in accordance with His character.

It is annoying, though, that Jonah does not seem to have learned a single lesson and is crankier than ever. Some critics conclude that Jonah could not possibly have written the book because it portrays him in such a bad light. Surely no respectable prophet would tarnish his public image with an exposé like this. Why would a man of God make himself look foolish on purpose?

For the Glory of God

The book of Jonah is a well-constructed piece of literature. Jonah relates his story so skillfully that the reader is hardly aware Jonah has made himself look foolish so we will side with God. Jonah, a great prophet who speaks directly with God, influences kings, and converts a major pagan city, has made sure we do not revere him. He knows his heart is sinful just like ours and he reveals his sin so we will honor God alone. Jonah makes sure no one finishes the book thinking, "What a great guy," but instead, "What a great God!"

Every turn in the plot and every display of Jonah's crankiness is designed to elicit a response from the reader. The more Jonah opposes God, the more we see the futility of his rebellion and the righteousness of God. In the end Jonah apparently remains a defiant sinner who refuses to repent. We, however, choose God's side. We solidly align ourselves with the sovereign, merciful Lord of the universe, worthy of all glory and honor.

Many scholars wisely conclude that Jonah could only have written such a brilliant apologetic for God's viewpoint if he were a faithful man of God who eventually acknowledged his sin and humbly repented after the events at Nineveh. Jesus speaks of Jonah not in terms of his disobedience but as a faithful prophet who serves as a type pointing to Christ.

Confessions

Jonah's humility and willingness to reveal his sin are echoed in the life of Saint Augustine, the esteemed Bishop of Hippo in North Africa. Around A.D. 400 Augustine wrote his *Confessions* disclosing certain sinful episodes from his youth.[32] In one incident he and his friends stole large amounts of fruit from a farmer's pear tree simply because it was forbidden. Critics denounced Augustine for diminishing his stature by writing about the foolish incident.

What critics missed was Augustine's analogy with Adam's sin in the Garden of Eden. Augustine was aware that if he had been in the Garden he would have chosen to sin just like Adam. Augustine humbly exposed his sinful nature so others would not imitate him but avoid his errors, repent, and turn to Christ for salvation. His *Confessions,* like the book of Jonah, confess his sinful heart and confess God's merciful and sovereign glory so we will respond in faith.

Part II: Studying Scripture

Read Jonah 4:6-11

1. God's Provision

God ordained or appointed four things for Jonah. The Hebrew verb does not necessarily imply that God prepared or created something new, but that He provided or supplied it. What four things did God ordain and was each one sent as a blessing or a curse?

1:17 _____

4:6 _____

4:7 _____

4:8 _____

2. God's Blessings

Jonah made a shelter for protection from the sun, but God graciously provided more effective shade. The Hebrew word for the ordained plant (*qiqayon*) has uncertain meaning. Some scholars think it is a castor oil plant with wide leaves and a supple stem easily destroyed by insect damage. Others think it is a fast-growing vine like a climbing gourd plant.

In v. 6, there is a double meaning. God is protecting Jonah physically from the sun "to save him from his discomfort." The same phrase could also be translated to mean God is blessing Jonah in order to encourage him to repent, "to deliver him from his evil." The plant is a double blessing.

a) Jonah is happy for the first and only time in the story. Until now the closest thing to joy was his gratefulness for being saved by the fish. In v. 6, what is Jonah exceedingly glad about?

b) This incident tells us something about Jonah's incomplete relationship with God. What does Jonah delight in with regard to God? What is lacking in Jonah's relationship with God?

c) How will you avoid Jonah's error, and rejoice in your relationship with God regardless of His material blessings?

3. God's Curses

Jonah only enjoyed the plant for one day. God withdrew His blessing by ordaining a worm that attacked the plant and made it wither. God also ordained a scorching hot "east wind," which may not literally have come from the east in this case. Some commentators suggest the wind was the *sirocco*, a hot Sahara wind that moves northward with hurricane force at times. Heat from the wind, sun, and lack of shade made Jonah quite sick.

a) In v. 7-9, why do you think God would destroy the shade plant that made Jonah happy? Why does Jonah's anger show that he still has a lot to learn about God's sovereign right to do as He pleases, particularly with regard to showing mercy and withholding mercy?

b) In v. 9, there is a subtle word-play in the Hebrew. The word for "angry" also means to be "hot." Jonah has intense anger over the withered plant and God sends intense heat. When has God had to turn up the heat, so to speak, to get your attention?

c) How will you develop a right relationship with God that does not depend on whether or not you like what God is doing?

d) Read Deuteronomy 28:2-6, 15-19. The covenant relationship between God and His people includes certain obligations. God promises blessings and curses depending on His people's hearts and behavior. In v. 2, what does God want from His people?

e) Read Jeremiah 29:11-14. God promised restoration for His people after the punishment of the Babylonian Exile. God would much rather send blessings than curses. Even when God has to punish His people, His goal is to bring them to repentance so their relationship with Him can be restored. What part of God's promises to the exiles do you find most comforting?

4. Choose Life

In v. 9, Jonah expresses a preference for death over life for the third time. Each time he chooses death, his anguish and despondency reveal an area where he is not willing to align his will with God's, as summarized in the chart below.

God's Will

God's Will for His People	Jonah's Opposition to God's Will
Obedience to God's word	Refusal to go to Nineveh (1:1-3, 12)
Mercy to repentant sinners	Anger at God's compassion (4:1-3)
Submission to God's sovereignty	Judgment that God is wrong (4:1-9)

---

a)   In which of the above areas have you been reluctant to align your will with God's? How has the struggle resulted in anguish or a lack of peace in your life?

b)   God sets before us a choice between life and death, blessings and curses. He wants us to choose life not only in a physical sense but also a spiritual sense:

> "I call heaven and earth to witness against you today, that I have set before you life and death, blessing and curse. Therefore choose life, that you and your offspring may live, *loving* the LORD your God, *obeying* his voice and *holding fast* to him, for he is your life and length of days..." (Deuteronomy 30:19-20, italics added)

Notice that God's advice to choose life relates to the three areas where Jonah refuses to align his will with God's will. Jonah would not have experienced such deep anguish about life if he had been willing to *obey* God's word; *love* God and thereby mercifully love people; and *hold fast* to God without judging God, in submission to His sovereignty.

How would you describe the positive difference it makes in your life when you live in accordance with God's will by obeying, loving and holding fast to Him? What has been affected most, your outward behavior or your inner attitude? How do unbelievers react to your contentment and zest for life?

c) Jesus came to give us eternal life. The term eternal life does not just refer quantitatively to never-ending life but also qualitatively to life in the kingdom of God which is available to us here and now in Christ. What are a few things the apostle John teaches about eternal life in the verses below?

John 10:10 _____

John 17:2 _____

John 17:3 _____

5. Choose Compassion

Jonah's anger about Nineveh's salvation turns into anger about the plant's demise. Since Jonah liked the material blessing of the plant, we might assume his anger is caused by the loss of shade, especially since Jonah became ill from the heat. However, when the plant dies the text indicates that Jonah is angry on behalf of the plant, not on his own behalf. This is surprising but encouraging. Jonah feels pity for the withered plant, not for himself.

The depth of Jonah's compassion for the plant is hidden by our translations that say the plant "came into being in a night" or "sprang up overnight." In v. 10, the original Hebrew says the "*ben* of a night became" and the "*ben* of a night perished."[33] Jonah thinks of the plant as a *ben*, meaning a son or child.

a) Even though Jonah did not do anything to make the plant live or grow, he looks on the dying plant with pity as if it were his son. The Hebrew word for "pity" denotes feeling that goes out toward someone who is in trouble. How is Jonah's pity for the withered plant commendable?

b) On the other hand, how would you contrast Jonah's pity for the plant with his lack of pity for the people of Nineveh? What trouble did the people of Nineveh face? In v. 11, how does God feel toward them?

c) Jonah's intense anger at God over killing the innocent plant is related to his intense anger at God over saving wicked Nineveh. Jonah struggles to understand why God shows mercy to the wicked while the innocent suffer. Where do you see people struggling with the same issue today? How will you learn to trust the goodness of God's sovereignty?

d) Jonah ignores the importance of repentance, whether it is wicked Nineveh's repentance or his own failure to repent. How will you avoid Jonah's error and express repentance as you seek to draw close to God?

6. God's Perfect Compassion

In v. 11, God says there are 120,000 people in Nineveh "who do not know their right hand from their left." Some scholars think this refers to children. That would indicate a word play here. Jonah pities his plant as if it were a child, but fails to pity the multitude of children in Nineveh who would have perished if he had not preached God's word.

Others think the number is much too large to refer to children, but may refer to the overall population. The fact that they cannot tell their right hand from their left might mean the people lacked moral perception. It is not that they were morally innocent, but that sin had made them spiritually blind.

a) The Ninevites' spiritual blindness meant they would never be able to turn to God on their own. God compassionately sent His prophet Jonah to save them by leading them to repentance. How is our sinful condition similar to theirs? Who did God mercifully send to save us?

b) God has the last word in the book, indicating He is not yet done with Jonah. While Jonah focuses on his single plant, God reminds him of the people and animals as well. Scripture affirms that animals are important to God (Genesis 1:30, 2:19) and people are even more important (Genesis 1:26-27). Jonah's vision is too narrow. He needs to lift his eyes from his plant to the big picture of God's love for the whole world. How can people learn to see their personal life and the world from God's broader viewpoint?

Part III: Personal Application and Growth

Today's lesson points to several important truths that apply to our personal lives. Allow these truths to penetrate your mind, soften your heart, deepen your faith and affect your behavior to help you continually grow in Christ.

1. We need to align our will with God's, particularly in the areas of obedience to His word, mercy to others, and submission to His sovereignty.

What practical changes will you make to align your will with God's will in areas where you struggle against Him?

2. Choose life by loving God, obeying His word, and holding fast to Him.

We were made for joyous, generous, abundant life, not just survival. It is a spiritual issue. How will you embrace abundant spiritual life in Christ this week? What do you think people will sense about you that is different?

3. Lift your eyes to the bigger picture and learn to see the world from God's point of view.

What is one step you will take to see life from God's broad point of view? What will be some of the benefits of shifting your focus from yourself and your immediate problems to the bigger picture?

Part IV: Closing Prayer

by John Calvin

Grant, Almighty God, that as we are loaded with so many vices and so many sins, yes, and scandalous crimes break out daily among us;

O grant that we may not be hardened against so many exhortations by which you invite us to yourself, but that being made contrite in spirit whenever you denounce on us your wrath we may be really humbled, and so place ourselves before your tribunal that we may, by a true confession and genuine fear, consider the judgment which would otherwise have been prepared for us;

And that in the meantime relying on Christ our Mediator, we may entertain such a hope of pardon as may raise us up to you; and not doubt but that you are ready to embrace us when we shall be moved by a true and real feeling of fear and penitence, since it is a proof of your favor when you are pleased to consider us, and when your Spirit testifies that you are a Father to us;

And, in a word, may we be so cast down in ourselves as to raise up our hope even to heaven, through Jesus Christ our Lord. Amen.[34]

❧ Lesson 8 ❧
Jesus and the Sign of Jonah
Matthew 12:38-42 and 16:1-4

Part I: Setting the Stage

Purpose
Our study of Jonah would be incomplete without looking at the way Jesus regards him in the New Testament. It is important for us to understand Jonah the way Christ did, and realize that Jonah was a great prophet whose life points us to salvation in Jesus Christ.

Look for the following application points in this lesson:

1. God is in control of the world and runs it every second of every day by His providence.
2. The kingdom of God has come into the world, but consummation of the kingdom is still to come.
3. There is no need to demand more proof of who Jesus is, for we have all the evidence we need recorded in Scripture.

Miracles and God's Providence
Jesus refers to Jonah after two separate miraculous events. In one episode Jesus heals a blind, mute, demon-possessed man. In the other Jesus heals and feeds a crowd of 4,000. Following each of these spectacular displays of power the religious leaders demand another miraculous sign. Jesus rebukes them saying they will only receive "the sign of Jonah."

God normally runs the world by His *ordinary providence*, meaning that He works through secondary causes such as the laws of nature He established. God sustains the world every second of every day and He is the sole reason the world continues to exist. If He were to withdraw His hand the result would be cosmic disaster. From the biggest to the smallest detail, our Creator God is the primary cause for everything in the universe and He actively provides for its continuing care in Christ (Colossians 1:15-17; Hebrews 1:3).

Sometimes God works by means of His *extraordinary providence.* He may directly cause things to happen without secondary causes, or He may interrupt secondary causes and use them in unusual ways. Miracles are unexpected, powerful demonstrations of God's extraordinary providence.[35]

The Purpose of Miracles

Miracles in the Bible authenticate both the person performing the miracle and the accompanying message as sent by God. The miracle reinforces the preaching of God's word. In the Old Testament, miracles most often appear in clusters at the time of Moses and the prophets, verifying them as people of God who reveal God's redemptive promises. In the New Testament, miracles authenticate Jesus and the apostles as bearers of the good news that God's redemptive promises are fulfilled in Jesus:

> "Men of Israel, hear these words: Jesus of Nazareth, a man attested to you by God with mighty works and wonders and signs that God did through him in your midst, as you yourselves know..." (Acts 2:22)

Mighty Works, Wonders and Signs

Interestingly, there is no word for miracle in ancient Hebrew and Greek. In our English Bibles the word miracle translates several Hebrew and Greek words. For instance, the word miracle may refer to power or mighty works (*geburah* in Hebrew; *dynamis* in Greek); wonders (*mopet* in Hebrew; *teras* in Greek); or a sign (*ot* in Hebrew; *semeion* in Greek).

In general, power and works refer to God's ability to perform a miracle (Deuteronomy 3:24; Luke 5:17). Wonders and marvels elicit a response of awe from the observer (Exodus 3:20; Acts 2:43). Signs point to God's authority and prove that the messenger speaks for God (Exodus 4:8; John 2:11).

Occasionally pagan magicians in Scripture manage to produce counterfeit miracles, but such false miracles are accompanied by false teaching. When the Jewish leaders claim that Jesus' miracles are from Satan, they are thereby asserting that Jesus is evil and His message is false. They demand a sign that will prove Jesus' authority is from God, but Jesus is aware there is no proof they will ever accept. Since they knowingly reject the truth, they bring condemnation on themselves.

Jesus performed sufficient miracles to prove to observers that He was from God. God's miracle of the resurrection was the ultimate evidence. Whether in the 1st century or 21st century, there is no need for further proof that Jesus is the Messiah, the Son of God, God Himself in the flesh.

Part II: Studying Scripture

Read Matthew 12:22-29, 38-42

1. Signs of the Kingdom of God

The kingdom of God (kingdom of heaven) was ushered into the world with the first coming of Jesus. However, the consummation of the kingdom is future and will not be complete until the second coming of Jesus at the end times. The coming of the kingdom of God is therefore both "already" and "not yet," also referred to as "realized" and "unrealized" eschatology.[36]

Author Nancy Pearcey describes the situation in military terms. God's world has been invaded and occupied by Satan and his minions who constantly wage war against God's people, but God entered the world in the person of Jesus Christ whose resurrection dealt Satan a fatal blow:

> "The outcome of the war is certain; yet the occupied territory has not actually been liberated. There is now a period where God's people are called to participate in

the follow-up battle, pushing the Enemy back... Between Christ's first and second coming, we must balance both the 'already' and the 'not yet' aspects of this interim phase."[37]

a) Signs of the Messiah's reign in the kingdom of God include divine restoration of sight and speech and the binding of Satan (Isaiah 35:5-6; Revelation 20:2). When Jesus healed the blind, mute, demon-oppressed man, therefore, He proved that the kingdom had entered the world. Jesus is in control, Satan is bound, and the world could be much worse off than it is. Where do you see evidence today that evil is restrained?

b) On the other hand, the kingdom of God is not yet consummated. We still live in a fallen world. Although Satan is bound, his demons and followers are active in the world. What evidence do you see today that evil still exists in the world?

2. The Sign of Jonah

The Pharisees were a special group of scribes. Scribes were Jewish lawyers, judges and rabbis who studied or taught religious law. The Pharisees separated themselves from ceremonially unclean people and things in order to strictly follow Mosaic Law. Common people admired them, but Jesus criticized the Pharisees for hypocritically violating the spirit of the law.

The Pharisees openly opposed Jesus. In v. 24, they accuse Jesus of working by the power of Satan (Beelzebul). In v. 38, they insult Jesus further by demanding another sign to prove His authority is from God. Their request is not sincere and Jesus responds by saying they will be given no other sign than "the sign of the prophet Jonah," meaning Jesus' burial and resurrection. Both Jonah and Jesus were held in the darkness of the fish or earth for three days and nights and God miraculously brought them forth alive.

Read the parallel passage in Luke 11:29-32. When the parallel passages are taken together as summarized below, we see two things. First, the sign of

Jonah is Jesus' burial and (implied) resurrection. Second, Jesus condemns the Pharisees for not believing the signs already given that confirm Jesus' wisdom and preaching, for even pagans believe God's signs of wisdom and preaching.

The Sign of Jonah: Resurrection

Matthew 12:38-42	Luke 11:29-32
No sign will be given	No sign will be given
but the sign of Jonah;	but the sign of Jonah;
for as Jonah was in the fish,	for as Jonah was a sign,
Jesus will be in the earth.	Jesus will be a sign.
The Ninevites repented	The Queen of Sheba listened
at Jonah's preaching;	to Solomon's wisdom;
the Queen of Sheba listened	the Ninevites repented
to Solomon's wisdom.	at Jonah's preaching.

---

a) Jesus takes Jonah seriously and recalls his greatness, not his disobedience. Jesus invokes Jonah during His argument against the Pharisees, a confrontation with deadly overtones. If the Pharisees cannot stop Jesus by defeating Him in public debate, how do they plan to stop Him? (See Matthew 12:14)

b) Why do you suppose the Pharisees would find it offensive for Jesus to say they will be judged by a pagan woman and wicked pagan men?

c) Jesus' resurrection was the ultimate miracle verifying His preaching and His atoning work on the cross. What did Jesus indicate about the possibility that the miracle of the resurrection would convince His enemies to believe His message of repentance and salvation? (See Luke 16:27-31)

d) How did the religious leaders actually react to the resurrection? (See Matthew 28:11-15)

e) Numerous frescoes in Roman catacombs show Jonah being spewed from a fish's mouth, representing resurrection. Why would Jonah be a sign of hope and comfort to persecuted Christians hiding in the catacombs? What mental picture of Jonah will you form to remind you of Jesus Christ and His resurrection?

3. Seeking God's Wisdom

a) The Pharisees came to Jesus seeking to discredit Him. In contrast, a thousand years earlier the Queen of Sheba came to King Solomon sincerely seeking wisdom. Sheba is probably Yemen, a distance of 1,200 miles south of Jerusalem. What had the queen heard about Solomon? (See I Kings 10:1)

b) Solomon's wealth and wisdom exceeded the queen's wildest expectations. She praised the LORD and gave Him credit for Solomon's success, reflecting Solomon's own attitude toward God at the time. What does the queen know about God because of Solomon's relationship with Him? (See I Kings 10:9)

4. Fulfillment in Jesus Christ

In Matthew 12, Jesus says He is greater than the Temple, Jonah, and Solomon. Notice that these comparisons involve the three main offices in

Israel: priest, prophet, and king. Jesus is the ultimate fulfillment of these offices and therefore He can teach God's people how to respond rightly to God.

a)   Jesus Is Greater Than the Temple

The priests who served in the Temple worshipped God with ritual sacrifices. In v. 6-7, according to Jesus, one greater than priests and Temple, how should God's people worship? (See also Micah 6:8)

b)   Jesus Is Greater Than Jonah

In v. 41, Jesus says the wicked pagans of Nineveh repented at the prophet Jonah's preaching. How, then, do you think God's people should respond to the preaching of God's Son, one greater than Jonah?

c)   Jesus Is Greater Than Solomon

In v. 42, Jesus says the Queen of the South (Sheba) travelled from the ends of the earth to hear King Solomon's godly wisdom. How diligently, then, should God's people seek out and submit to the wisdom and authority of God's Son, one greater than Solomon?

Read Matthew 15:29-16:4

5. Another Demand for a Sign

Jesus' second reference to the sign of Jonah follows miraculous healings and the feeding of 4,000 people. The Pharisees and Sadducees demand that Jesus perform yet another miraculous sign to prove He is authorized by God. The Sadducees were the ruling priests of the Jewish council called the Sanhedrin, which was made up of high priests, scribes, tribal elders, and wealthy, aristocratic men.

The religious leaders had come from Jerusalem to test Jesus. Their demand for another miracle from heaven reminds us of Satan's testing of Jesus in the wilderness when Satan demanded a miracle from heaven (Matthew 4:6). Jesus accuses the leaders of failing to recognize the "signs of the times," meaning the powerful miracles He has already performed. If the leaders are not convinced by those miracles, another one will not make any difference. Therefore, Jesus will not provide another miracle for these wicked people except "the sign of Jonah" (resurrection).

a) What is sinful about demanding that God prove Himself to our satisfaction by providing us with a miraculous sign upon our request?

b) When have you been tempted to tell God how He can prove Himself to you? How will you learn to be content with what He has already revealed in Scripture and in your life?

6. The Evidence Today

a) In the crowd there were people who recognized Jesus as the Son of David, a term for the Messiah (Matthew 12:23). No one back then and no one today can remain neutral in response to meeting Jesus. What does Jesus say about neutrality in Luke 11:23? What is your response to Jesus?

b) Sometimes today unbelievers demand that we prove the trustworthiness of the Bible's testimony about Jesus Christ. The question we might ask them is, "What evidence are you willing to accept?" Many people are like the Pharisees and Sadducees; there really is no proof they want to accept concerning Jesus. Why do you think some people impose impossible standards of proof when it comes to the Bible, but not to other ancient writings?[38]

c) Who is Jesus Christ to you? What evidence regarding Christ is compelling to you?

Part III: Personal Application and Growth

Today's lesson points to several important truths that apply to our personal lives. Allow these truths to penetrate your mind, soften your heart, deepen your faith and affect your behavior to help you continually grow in Christ.

1. God is in control of the world and runs it every second of every day by His providence.

God created and actively maintains nature and the laws by which it operates. Since nature is a created thing under God's control, He can interrupt its laws to suit His purposes. With this understanding, explain why it is reasonable to accept the existence of Biblical miracles. Practice stating your explanation so you will be ready to answer a skeptic who denies miracles.

2. The kingdom of God has come into the world, but consummation of the kingdom is still to come.

The concept of "the already and the not yet" puts evil in proper perspective. We must deal with evil in this lifetime, yet Jesus Christ has already dealt Satan a fatal blow and the ultimate outcome is decided. How will you draw comfort and confidence from this truth when sin impacts your life this week?

3. There is no need to demand more proof of who Jesus is, for we have all the evidence we need recorded in Scripture.

The Bible is where we learn that Jesus is the Son of God and we find the details of Jesus' moral teaching. Scripture is a unity and these truths cannot be separated. We must not judge God's word by accepting one truth about

Jesus and rejecting others. How will you answer people who say Jesus is a great moral teacher but not the Son of God?

Part IV: Closing Prayer

by John Calvin

Grant, Almighty God, that as you have in various ways testified, and daily continue to testify, how dear and precious to you are mankind, and as we enjoy daily so many and so remarkable proofs of your goodness and favor;

O grant that we may learn to rely wholly on your goodness, many examples of which you set before us, and which you would have us continually to experience, that we may not only pass through our earthly course, but also confidently aspire to the hope of that blessed and celestial life which is laid up for us in heaven, through Christ our Lord. Amen.[39]

SECTION II

THE PROPHET HABAKKUK

❧ Lesson 9 ❦
Habakkuk's First Complaint
Habakkuk 1:1-11

Please take time to read all three chapters of the book of Habakkuk to get an overview. As you read, notice that Habakkuk eventually submits to God's sovereignty, unlike Jonah. We are to imitate Habakkuk's model of faith.

Part I: Setting the Stage

Purpose
This lesson introduces us to the prophet Habakkuk's candid conversations with God. It is important for us to know that God wants His people to come to Him honestly with their concerns, praying boldly and respectfully.

Look for the following application points in this lesson:

1. God wants us to speak to Him candidly, boldly, and respectfully.
2. Faithful waiting for God's justice is active waiting:

> Trust in God's unfailing love
> Rejoice in God's salvation
> Sing of God's goodness
> Look at the bigger picture
> Be astounded at what God is doing
> Believe God's word

3. We should prepare ourselves spiritually in good times so we can face unexpected problems.

Author of the Book of Habakkuk

The opening verse identifies the author as the prophet Habakkuk. Habakkuk is not mentioned elsewhere in the Bible. The meaning of his name is uncertain but might be "to embrace," signifying that he embraces the Lord or the Lord embraces him. Or it might be from the Assyrian plant *hambakuku*, an indication that the Assyrian language had made its way into Judah's culture.

Date

No date is given for the book's composition, but it might have been written around 605 B.C. when the southern kingdom of Judah was being threatened by a rising foreign power, the Babylonians. This would place Habakkuk's ministry in Judah about one hundred fifty years after Jonah's ministry in Israel.

Contemporaries

The prophets Jeremiah, Zephaniah and Nahum also prophesied in Judah in the 7th century B.C. and perhaps were contemporaries with Habakkuk.

Audience

Habakkuk's oracle, literally "burden," was meant for the people in the southern kingdom of Judah. The first deportation of Jews into the Babylonian Exile may have already taken place, but not yet the final destruction of Jerusalem.

Social conditions in Judah were increasingly characterized by injustice, destruction, violence, strife and conflict under the rule of King Jehoiakim who actively overturned the religious and civil reforms of his father, the good King Josiah. The political and moral condition of the nation was in grave jeopardy as the people ignored God while expecting His continued covenant blessings.

Themes

Some important themes in the book of Habakkuk are listed below. This study considers theodicy to be the main theme as in the book of Jonah. A theodicy is an explanation of God's actions with regard to evil in light of His goodness.

Theodicy	*God is too pure to tolerate wrong (1:13)*
God's Grace	*May God in wrath remember mercy (3:2)*
Salvation	*God delivers His people (3:13)*
Faith	*Rejoice in God no matter what (3:17-18)*
God's Sovereignty	*The sovereign Lord is our strength (3:19)*

Outline

One of the challenging tasks for translators is to decide whether God or Habakkuk is speaking in various sections. The speaker changes without notice and sometimes pronouns have no clear referent. Translators place headings in our Bibles to identify who they think is speaking, but Bible versions may differ from each other. The following is a typical outline. Notice that God does not need to respond to Habakkuk a third time like He did with Jonah (see the outline for Jonah in Lesson 3, Part I).

Chapter 1:1-11	Habakkuk's first complaint and God's response
Chapter 1:12-2:20	Habakkuk's second complaint and God's response
Chapter 3	Habakkuk's prayer of faith

Part II: Studying Scripture

Read Habakkuk 1:1-4 .

Like Jonah, Habakkuk is a *navi*, literally "called one," the usual term for a prophet. He is a spokesperson for God. However, one of the unique aspects of the book of Habakkuk is that we only have the prophet's conversations with God rather than with people. Habakkuk asks God some hard questions and we find ourselves eager to know how God will respond. Habakkuk is not afraid to point out that his beliefs about God's just character don't match the reality of God's actions in the world.

1. Speaking Candidly

God wants us to bring all our concerns to Him, but we are to do so with respect for who He is. The Reformer John Calvin points out that Habakkuk gave full vent to his feelings within appropriate limits, and we should do the same:

> "Since God allows us to deal so familiarly with Him, nothing wrong ought to be ascribed to our prayers when we thus freely pour forth our feelings, provided the bridle of obedience keeps us always within due limits."[40]

a) What does it mean to keep within due limits when we pray?

b) In v. 2-3, what are four of Habakkuk's complaints about God's ways?

c) When have you felt like Habakkuk and how did you handle it?

d) We should allow God to use us as His instruments in confronting corruption in our culture. Ministry leader Joni Eareckson Tada compares corruption to the smog that so often covers Los Angeles:

> "We tend to forget that we live under a thick layer of moral corruption. We are no longer shocked by it... we just go about breathing our culture in and out without hardly noticing. 'It is what it is,' we say.

> "But I have noticed – and maybe you have, too – that Christians are more alert than ever before. We are beginning to understand that this age is ripe with opportunity. I've noticed that more Christians than ever are open to discussing the problems... Now is the time to shine light, shake salt, and tell people that Jesus Christ is our hope, and show them that the Bible offers answers."[41]

In what ways will you act as salt and light in Christ's name starting today?

2. Does God Care?

a) In v. 2, Habakkuk asks God the age-old lament, "How long?" This is apparently not the first time Habakkuk has cried out to God about His failure to deal with the wickedness of Judah. When have you asked God "How long?" Why do we ask God this question?

b) Read Psalm 13:1-6 where King David cries out to God, "How long?" David points out three ways we can demonstrate our faith while waiting for justice. Give an example of times when you have done these:

> Trust in God's unfailing love
> Rejoice in God's salvation
> Sing of God's goodness

c) Read Revelation 6:10-11 where the souls of martyrs in heaven cry out, "How long?" while waiting for God's justice. What answer do they receive? How do you feel knowing God has a plan, and history is moving forward with purpose? How does it reassure you to know God will accomplish perfect justice through Jesus Christ?

3. Righteous Indignation

In v. 4, Habakkuk cries out on behalf of innocent victims, not on his own behalf. John Calvin makes the comment,

> "This passage teaches us that all who really serve and love God ought, according to the Prophet's example, to burn with holy indignation whenever they see wickedness reigning without restraint among men, and especially in the Church of God."[42]

a) The law in Judah had been perverted so that justice could not prevail. What happens to society when the authority of law is ignored, or when those who should interpret and enforce the law put their own personal gain first?

b) What problems today do you think individual Christians should speak out against more passionately, whether the problems are in society or in the church? What responsibility does the local church have to speak out?

c) Why is it a sign of an unhealthy Christian life when a believer is not troubled by injustice and corruption, especially when the victims are poor and defenseless? What kind of constructive action will you take to help make a difference, motivated by your godly outrage and compassion?

Read Habakkuk 1:5-11

4. Active and Faithful Waiting

In v. 5, God tells Habakkuk to do three things while he is waiting for justice. These complement the acts of faith from Psalm 13 discussed above:

> Look at the bigger picture
> Be astounded at what God is doing
> Believe God's word

a) Habakkuk complains about having to "see iniquity" in Judah, but God redirects his eyes to "look among the nations." God gives him a new perspective. Why is it helpful for us to look with faith beyond the details of our immediate problems to see the bigger picture?

b) What do you think would astound you if you looked at world events through eyes of faith? How will you get better at seeing God's providence in events?

c) God says that Habakkuk wouldn't believe what God is doing even if he were told, and then God tells him. Why do we find it hard to believe God's word? Read Hebrews 2:1; 3:15. What practical advice does the author of Hebrews give with regard to believing God's word?

d) The apostle Paul quotes v. 5 at the end of his famous synagogue speech at Pisidian Antioch (Acts 13:40-41). He tells the Jews God is doing something they will never believe, meaning, of course, salvation in Christ. Paul warns them not to reject Jesus and thus bring judgment upon themselves. Being God's chosen people will not keep them safe from God's judgment any more than it kept Judah safe in Habakkuk's day. Why do you think so many people today do not take the warning of God's judgment seriously?

5. Accepting God's Sovereignty

As with Jonah, God does not owe Habakkuk any explanations. However, God answers Habakkuk's complaints in order to prepare him for what is coming. God knows it will be a shock to hear that Babylon, a nation more wicked than Judah, will be His instrument to punish Judah, God's chosen people.

a) God is sovereign over the rise and fall of all nations (Job 12:23). In v. 6, what phrase affirms that wicked Babylon (the Chaldeans) will not rise to power merely by human effort or chance?

b) The nations are under God's control and He uses them as instruments to accomplish His good purposes. In v. 6-7, what are a few things Judah should expect from the Babylonians, God's instrument of punishment?

6. Facing God's Judgment

In v. 8, God warns that the Jews should not count on the great distance between Babylon and Judah for safety. The Babylonian army could advance on horseback with amazing speed and ferocity. By day they move swiftly like leopards. By night they are like wolves, nocturnal predators that tear apart their prey and gorge themselves through the night. They are like eagles or vultures.

a) What do these vivid images tell us about the Babylonian army's purpose?

b) The Babylonians took the Jews into exile in Babylon in three major deportations. In v. 9, what image describes the large numbers of prisoners that would be taken? How many were taken in the second and largest deportation (see II Kings 24:14)?

c) In v. 10, how effective will Judah and other nations' defenses be against the Babylonians?

d) In v. 11, military strength had become a god to the Babylonians. What other types of strength can be a god or idol to a nation? How can nations avoid reliance on false gods?

e) The motto "In God We Trust" first appeared on U.S. coins in 1864 during the Civil War. Why does religious sentiment so often increase with the threat or reality of war?

f) Why should we spiritually prepare ourselves in the peaceful times of our lives to face unexpected crises instead of waiting until a problem appears?

Part III: Personal Application and Growth

Today's lesson points to several important truths that apply to our personal lives. Allow these truths to penetrate your mind, soften your heart, deepen your faith and affect your behavior to help you continually grow in Christ.

1. God wants us to speak to Him candidly, boldly, and respectfully.

Every day brings events in our lives or in the news that can evoke passionate, angry responses from us. What words will you use that show restraint and respect for God when you take strong negative feelings to Him in prayer? How will the practice of restraint help you grow in spiritual maturity?

2. Faithful waiting for God's justice is active waiting:

> Trust in God's unfailing love
> Rejoice in God's salvation
> Sing of God's goodness
> Look at the bigger picture
> Be astounded at what God is doing
> Believe God's word

Which of the above activities are easiest for you to do while waiting for God's justice? Which are you least likely to do? How will you incorporate all six into your waiting time to strengthen your faith?

3. We should prepare ourselves spiritually in good times so we can face unexpected problems.

People who wait for a crisis before turning to God find themselves at a loss for how to talk to God in prayer or hear from Him in Scripture. What steps will you take this week to develop your spiritual habits of prayer and Bible reading, both in terms of quantity and quality of time?

Part IV: Closing Prayer

by John Calvin

Grant, Almighty God, that since you set around us so many terrors, we may know that we ought to be roused and to resist the sloth and tardiness of our flesh, so that you may fortify us by a different confidence;

And may we so rest on your aid that we may boldly triumph over our enemies, and never doubt but that you will at length give us the victory over all the assaults of Satan and of the wicked;

And may we also so look to you that our faith may wholly rest on that eternal and immutable covenant which has been confirmed for us by the blood of your only Son, until we shall at length be united to Him who is our head, after having passed through all the miseries of the present life, and having been gathered into that eternal inheritance which your Son has purchased for us by His own blood. Amen.[43]

ఈ Lesson 10 ಈ
Habakkuk's Second Complaint
Habakkuk 1:12-2:1

Part I: Setting the Stage

Purpose

This lesson examines Habakkuk's second complaint to God. Habakkuk could not make sense out of God's plan to punish Judah by sending the Babylonians, a nation even more wicked than Judah. Babylon's reputation for merciless warfare terrifies Habakkuk, but he finally humbly submits to God's plan. It is important for us, like Habakkuk, to trust God's good purposes even when we cannot understand His ways.

Look for the following application points in this lesson:

1. God is the great I AM, the Creator, the Holy One of Israel, and our Rock.
2. Even in the darkest hours of history God saves a remnant of true believers, because His church, Christ's body, will always be present in the world.
3. We can wait patiently and confidently for God's justice, trusting His perfect ways.

Babylon and the Akkadian Empire

God is in control of the rise and fall of all nations and empires in history, including Babylon. Earliest records refer to Babylon as part of the Akkadian empire in Mesopotamia. Babylon was probably built up from a small town to a city-state around 2300 B.C.

Amorite Period

The Akkadian empire gradually weakened and its declining population was replaced around 2000 B.C. by two people groups. Assyrians moved into northern Mesopotamia and nomadic Amorites occupied Babylon and southern Mesopotamia. The Amorites were not unified, which allowed the city-state of Babylon to grow in its own power. In the meantime, around 2000 B.C. the Hebrew patriarch Abraham (Abram) moved from Mesopotamia to Canaan.

Old Babylonian Empire (1792-1595 B.C.)

Babylon emerged as an empire around 1800 B.C. under King Hammurabi, known for his law code. This first great Babylonian empire lasted two hundred years until it was defeated by Hittites from the north. In the meantime, the Hebrews were enslaved in Egypt for four hundred years, a period that extended before and after the Old Babylonian Empire.

Middle Babylonian Empire

The second Babylonian empire was founded by the Kassites, an Elamite tribe that may have come from the mountains east of Babylon. Although the Kassite dynasty lasted over five hundred years, very little is known about it. The Kassites were defeated by Assyria in 1115 B.C. In the meantime, the Israelites left Egypt in the Exodus and settled in Canaan as a loose confederacy of tribes governed by judges.

Assyrian Period

During the 11th and 10th centuries B.C. new peoples entered Mesopotamia. Those in the south were called Chaldeans, an ethnic term that eventually referred to Babylonians in general. The Assyrians in the north became the dominant power in the 8th century B.C. with the sudden rise of Tiglath-Pileser III (745 B.C.), not long after the prophet Jonah's ministry.

In the meantime, near the end of the 11th century B.C. Israel became a monarchy. After a hundred years the united kingdom of Israel divided into the kingdoms of Israel and Judah. Israel was destroyed by Assyria in 722 B.C. and Judah was reduced to a vassal state.

Neo-Babylonian Empire (626-539 B.C.)

Assyria grew weak through constant warfare. In 626 B.C. a new Babylonian empire was established by Nabopolassar. He defeated the Assyrian capital of Nineveh in 612 B.C. His son Nebuchadnezzar II came to the throne in 605 B.C. and expanded the empire, invading Judah and taking many Jews into exile in Babylon. The Babylonian empire could not be maintained, though, and it fell to Cyrus of Persia in 539 B.C., only 87 years after it began. Cyrus allowed the exiled Jews to return home to Judah.

In the meantime, sometime after 626 B.C. when Nabopolassar rose to power in Babylon, Habakkuk received his prophetic call in Judah. God revealed to Habakkuk that He would bring the distant Babylonians to punish Judah.

Part II: Studying Scripture

Read Habakkuk 1:12-17

Habakkuk's first complaint was that God had not punished Judah's sin, but his second complaint is that God's punishment will be too harsh. Habakkuk still does not think God is acting in accord with His righteous character.

1. God's Sovereignty

a) Habakkuk wisely begins his second complaint by acknowledging who God is and His right to ordain judgment. In v. 12, he addresses God with four different names. What aspects of God's sovereignty does each name reflect?[44]

LORD (*Yahweh*): _____

God (*Elohim*): _____

Holy One: _____

Rock: _____

b) If you were faced with a sudden crisis, which of the above names for God would you most likely use while praying to Him? Why?

c) Although Habakkuk knows God has the sovereign right to ordain any punishment He chooses for Judah, Habakkuk does not like God's plan. He points out why God should not use the Babylonians to punish Judah. What is so loathsome about the Babylonians with regard to the following:

Morality (1:13) _____

Worship (1:16) _____

Conquest (1:17) _____

2. God's Remnant

Despite the coming Babylonian invasion, Habakkuk is confident that God will save a remnant of believers. In v. 12, he cries out with confidence, "We shall not die," knowing that although there will certainly be death and destruction, God will save a remnant of believers. God always saves a remnant somewhere in the world in every age. He will never let His people die out completely and leave the world without a witness to Him. The church is the remnant of believers in the world today, the true Israel (Romans 11:1-7).

a) Centuries earlier the prophet Elijah needed reassurance there was a remnant of believers. Elijah had successfully defeated the prophets of Baal, but had to run for his life. He cried out that he was the only believer left in Israel. God told Elijah to get on with his work, and then assured him there were thousands of believers in Israel (I Kings 19:14-18). When we feel alone in our faith like Elijah, perhaps because of hostility from our family or culture, what do you think God expects us to do, like He expected of Elijah?

b) It can be disheartening for Christians to see the rise of secular humanism and other false religions. Even though Christianity has survived similar dark periods in history, it can seem that the truth about Christ will soon be lost forever. How does it encourage you to know that God always saves a remnant of true believers?

c) Theologian R. B. Kuiper reminds us that the church will never be destroyed because the body of Christ cannot be destroyed; it will continue to grow to completion:

> "God will at all times have a covenant people, a church, on earth... Ours is an age of rapid dechristianization of the Christian nations. It might seem that the inevitable outcome will be the ruination of the Christian church. Not so. The faithful, covenant God has promised that at least a remnant will be preserved. That remnant will never fail to proclaim the glad tidings of salvation to a lost world... God will keep adding to the church until all His elect from every nation shall have been brought in."[45]

3. The Wicked: Disregard for Human Dignity

In v. 14-15, Habakkuk employs fishing imagery to illustrate how easily the Babylonians will capture the Jews. He laments that God has ordained His people to be like fish in the sea.

a) What are the implications of being like sea creatures that have no ruler?

b) The Babylonians generally caught fish with baskets and large nets, using hooks to drag nets or hang fish together. A Babylonian relief shows conquerors dragging their enemies in fishnets. Both the Babylonians and Assyrians were known to drive a hook through the lower lip or nose of their captives and string them along in single file.[46] Why would a conqueror treat captives this way?

c) Treating people like fish, even in wartime, violates the inherent human dignity of both the captives and their conquerors. All humans are created in the image of God. In our culture, in what areas would you say there should be more respect for human dignity and worth?

4. The Wicked: Idolatry

a) The Babylonians were polytheistic, meaning they worshiped more than one god. Bel Marduk was the supreme god of the Babylonian pantheon of gods.[47] In v. 16, what phrases show that the Babylonians also idolized their military strength, represented by nets, for the plunder and prosperity it provided?

b) People have always been tempted to idolize and worship created things instead of acknowledging the Creator God as the source of all blessing. Why does prosperity so often lead to idolatry? How will you learn to enjoy God's blessings of prosperity while avoiding idolatry?

c) In v. 17, Habakkuk wonders if Babylon is to "keep on emptying his net," conquering and plundering indefinitely. In one sense Habakkuk accuses God of ordaining unfair excessive punishment. In another sense Habakkuk accuses God of tolerating increased idolatry, for the more Babylon conquers and prospers, the more its idolatry grows. Why do you suppose God has allowed so many idolatrous, pagan nations to rise to power at various times in history and today?

5. The Wicked: Undeserved Prosperity

Habakkuk does not doubt God's righteous character and sovereignty, but he is perplexed as to how a righteous God could be willing to tolerate or use evil to accomplish His good purposes. God is too pure and holy to tolerate evil, yet God evidently does tolerate evil, at least for a time.

a) Read Psalm 73:1-5. It does not seem fair that wicked people prosper. The psalmist complains that the wicked generally achieve health and wealth while the righteous suffer. However, when the psalmist turns to God in worship, God reveals the truth to him. In Psalm 73:27, what is the destiny of the wicked?

b) God does not reveal the destiny of the wicked Babylonians to Habakkuk quite yet. Why do you think God waits to reveal the Babylonians' eventual downfall until Habakkuk is willing to conform his will to God's?

c) In v. 4 Habakkuk complained about Judah's wickedness, but in v. 13 he calls them righteous compared to the wicked Babylonians. What is the spiritual danger of downplaying our sin by comparing ourselves favorably to people that are more sinful? How will you avoid downplaying your sin and your need for Christ?

Read Habakkuk 2:1

6. The Faithful: Standing at the Watchpost

Habakkuk decides to wait confidently and patiently for God's answer to his second complaint, whatever the answer will be. Habakkuk will stand as if he were a guard on the ramparts of Jerusalem watching attentively for a messenger. What a contrast to Jonah who sat in defiant anger, waiting for God to see things his way (Jonah 4:5). Pastor D. A. Carson observes,

> "Christians who have no answers to why this or that happened can afford to take the long view. The God they know is a just God; He will ensure that justice is done... That means they do not always have ready answers; they have, instead, a reasonable confidence in One who does have the answers and the power to impose them. God will have the last word; we dare to wait for that."[48]

a) Contrast Habakkuk's earlier frustration about God's apparent failure to hear his complaint (1:2) with his confidence that God indeed hears him (2:1). What do you suppose brought about Habakkuk's new outlook?

b) The military language of 2:1 hints that Habakkuk is now less interested in criticizing God and more interested in obeying God like a loyal soldier, whether he understands Him or not. How is this a major turning point in Habakkuk's faith journey, as it should be in ours?

c) Habakkuk was not the only one waiting. God had been waiting, too, for His people's repentance. When it looks to us like God fails to bring justice, He might instead be mercifully waiting for sinners to come to repentance. How will this perspective help you to be more patient and respond in faith while you wait for God to bring justice?

d) We can go to our watchpost to pray while we wait patiently for God to act in our lives, but we should not expect God to speak directly to us the same way He spoke to the prophets. Scripture is the way God speaks to us today, and we hear God's word when we read the Bible. Why are small group Bible studies an effective way to stay in God's word?

e) Author Nancy DeMoss reminds us,

> "God speaks clearly today, as clearly as ever, by His Spirit and through His written Word, the Bible, so do not expect God to speak to you or to answer you when you go to your watchpost... God is not revealing anything new today. He's given us all we need to know. Now, the Holy Spirit will take this Word, quicken it to our hearts... show you how it should be applied to your current life circumstances and situation."[49]

Part III: Personal Application and Growth

Today's lesson points to several important truths that apply to our personal lives. Allow these truths to penetrate your mind, soften your heart, deepen your faith and affect your behavior to help you continually grow in Christ.

1. God is the great I AM, the Creator, the Holy One of Israel, and our Rock.

Do you think of God more in terms of His holiness (transcendence) or His nearness (immanence)? When you pray, what specific words will you use to address both of these aspects of God's being? How will you grow in faith as you honor both aspects?

2. Even in the darkest hours of history God saves a remnant of true believers, because His church, Christ's body, will always be present in the world.

As Europe and North America become increasingly secular and spiritually dark, we can at least be encouraged that the gospel is spreading in other parts of the world. As part of God's remnant, the church, what practical step will you take this week to be a light shining the gospel truth in your corner of the world?

3. We can wait patiently and confidently for God's justice, trusting His perfect ways.

We might wait a lifetime and still not see God's justice prevail in certain circumstances, but we must continue to trust that God will prevail in the end. In what tangible way will you demonstrate your trust in God's justice and timing this week? How will your attitude encourage other people?

Part IV: Closing Prayer

by John Calvin

Grant, Almighty God, that as you see us laboring under so much weakness, yes, with our minds so blinded that our faith falters at the smallest perplexities, and almost fails altogether;

O grant that by the power of your Spirit we may be raised up above this world, and learn more and more to renounce our own counsels, and so to come to you, that we may stand fixed in our watch tower, ever hoping through your power for whatever you have promised to us, though you might not immediately make it manifest to us that you have faithfully spoken;

And may we thus give full proof of our faith and patience, and proceed in the course of our warfare until at length we ascend above all watch towers into that blessed rest, where we shall no more watch with an attentive mind, but see face to face in your image whatever can be wished, and whatever is needful for our perfect happiness, through Christ our Lord. Amen.[50]

๕ Lesson 11 ๖
The Justice of God
Habakkuk 2:2-20

Part I: Setting the Stage

Purpose
Today's lesson wrestles with the question of why a good God allows evil in the world. Is God somehow not fair, just, good or powerful enough to overcome evil? People have struggled with this question throughout the ages. God assures Habakkuk that He is in control of evil and will not let it continue forever. It is important for us to know that God has His good reasons for allowing evil for a while even if we do not understand those reasons.

Look for the following application points in this lesson:

1. We are to trust that God is good, powerful, and just, and has a morally sufficient reason for allowing evil to exist in the world.
2. The righteous will live by faith in Christ's saving work.
3. Our lives are to honor and reflect the splendor of God's radiant glory.

The Problem of Evil
One reason unbelievers say they cannot believe in God or Christianity is called "the problem of evil." The problem is usually presented somewhat like this:

Premise #1: God is all-good and should conquer evil.
Premise #2: God is all-powerful and is able to conquer evil.

Conclusion: Therefore, since evil exists, God is either not all-good or not all-powerful.

Christians should understand that the premises are correct but the conclusion is faulty. It is not necessary to conclude that God is not good or powerful when He allows evil to exist for a time. God is in control of everything, including evil. God has good reasons for allowing evil to exist whether we comprehend His reasons or not. It is enough for us to know that God's reasons for allowing evil are consistent with His moral character.

We do not have to let the unbelieving world define the terms of the discussion. God is good and He is sovereign over evil. We may not understand God's reasons for allowing evil, but our lack of understanding should not lead us to diminish His character, power, or saving work in Jesus Christ. Let us replace the unbeliever's conclusion with the following conclusion based on faith:[51]

Conclusion: Therefore, since evil exists, God must have a morally sufficient reason to allow it.

A Problem for Unbelievers
Ironically, the problem of evil is a philosophical problem for unbelievers more than believers. Without God, unbelievers cannot speak meaningfully about good and evil. If morality is determined by society or anyone other than God, then good and evil become a matter of mere preference or opinion. There can be no problem of evil if there is no real good or evil. The discussion ends.

No matter what they say, though, unbelievers act and live as if there is a universal moral code that informs standards of good and evil. Certain behaviors such as murder or the abuse of children are deemed inherently wrong. The truth is that God has written His moral code on everyone's heart whether they acknowledge Him or not. There is such a thing as good and evil.

Theodicy: What Is God's Reason for Allowing Evil?
Having concluded that good and evil exist, and that God has a morally sufficient reason for allowing evil, we are left with a follow-up question:

What is God's reason? This takes us into the search for a theodicy (the justification of God's actions with regard to evil in light of His goodness). One reasonable theodicy is called the greater-good defense which says that God allows evil in order to bring about a better world for His glory. The chief example of the greater-good defense is the cross of Jesus. If God can bring good out of an evil situation like the cross, He can be trusted to bring good out of the evils in our lives and the world today.

Although theodicies explain God's actions to a certain extent, in the end we are still left with mystery. We do not know exactly why God allows evil and suffering in certain cases, how His actions contribute to the greater good, or how He accomplishes His purposes. Theologian John Frame reminds us that the ultimate theodicy or explanation is future, not in this lifetime:

> "It is not necessary for us to come up with a full theodicy,
> a complete justification of God's ways. In this world, we
> walk by faith, not by sight."[52]

Habakkuk arrives at the same conclusion. When he cannot understand God's ways, he accepts God's declaration that "the righteous will live by his faith." May we imitate Habakkuk's faith by trusting God to be just and merciful.

Part II: Studying Scripture

Read Habakkuk 2:2-5

1. God's Reassurance

In v. 2, God responds to Habakkuk's complaint about the Babylonians by telling him to expect a vision. God tells him to write it plainly on tablets, not scrolls, so it will be easy to read at a glance. Depending on how the verse is translated, either a herald is to carry the tablets and read out loud as he runs, or people are to read the message as they hurry past. The message is not just for Habakkuk, but for the edification of all God's people for generations to come.

In v. 3, a few commentators say God's revelation is the punishment of Judah described in the previous chapter. However, Habakkuk expects revelation that he has not yet heard. Most commentators therefore conclude that the revelation is God's condemnation of the Babylonians to be described more fully in this chapter. The end of Babylon will occur in due time and Judah is to wait patiently for it, looking forward to it.

a) The Babylonians were not defeated until 539 B.C., many decades after Habakkuk's vision. How would v. 3 have reassured Jews who were living in exile in Babylon during those years?

b) Think of a situation where you wonder if God will ever bring justice. How will it serve as an encouragement to you to know that God's justice is not delayed, even if it seems slow? How will you learn to be content knowing that God's justice may not be accomplished in your lifetime, but it will happen?

2. God's Righteous One

In v. 4, God contrasts the arrogant Babylonians with the pious believer who relies on God: "the righteous shall live by his faith." Jewish tradition taught that this phrase summarized the 613 laws of the Torah (Pentateuch). The idea of living by faith was grounded in the Old Testament and continued in the New, notably in the writings of the apostle Paul. Since Habakkuk influenced Paul who influenced the Reformers Luther and Calvin, Habakkuk has been nicknamed "the great-grandfather of the Reformation."

a) Paul utilizes v. 4 as the basis for understanding the gospel (Romans 1:16-17; Galatians 3:11). He emphasizes the word *righteous*, giving it a legal meaning in the sense of measuring up to God's holy standards.[53] We are righteous only because of Christ's work on the cross whereby He imputes His righteousness to us, and God graciously counts it as our own.[54] How should we respond to the good news that our righteousness is by God's grace?

b) The Reformer Martin Luther's understanding of righteousness was based on Paul. Luther's insistence that our righteousness and salvation are by God's grace alone was at the heart of the Reformation. Luther comments on Paul's letter to the Romans,

> "[With regard to salvation] works are a total loss and are completely useless. That is what St. Paul means in Chapter 3 when he says, 'No human being is justified before God through the works of the law'... Grace does do this much: that we are accounted completely righteous before God."[55]

Since our good works count as nothing toward our righteousness and salvation, but are an expression of our gratitude, how will you overflow in good works?

c) The Reformer John Calvin's understanding of righteousness was also based on Paul. Commenting on Paul's letter to the Romans, Calvin says,

> "If we seek salvation, that is, life with God, righteousness must be first sought... Righteousness is offered by the gospel and is received by faith... We are made righteous by faith through the grace of God alone."[56]

How will you explain grace to someone who thinks they just need to do more good deeds than bad ones in order to earn salvation and go to heaven?

d) The author of the book of Hebrews quotes v. 4 with an emphasis on the word *faith*. He encourages believers to persevere in faith despite persecution because God's timing is perfect and Christ will come without delay at the right time as promised (Hebrews 10:36-38). Why do we have trouble trusting that God's timing is perfect? Why do you suppose God does not tell us everything about His timing and plans?

When have you been glad that God did not reveal His timing to you beforehand?

3. Babylon's Arrogance

a)   In v. 4-5, how does God describe the wicked Babylonians?

b)   Why is it true in general that the wicked can never get enough and are never satisfied? What is their underlying spiritual problem?

c)   Even godly people can have trouble defining what is enough. It is easy to get drawn into an unhealthy desire for more and more through constant exposure to advertising. What will you do to define what is enough for you?

Read Habakkuk 2:6-20

4. Babylon's Doom

God assures Habakkuk that Babylon will not continue to ravage the nations forever. God's vision sets forth five taunting woes of judgment against Babylon's wickedness. He promises retribution and says that one day those persecuted by Babylon will exult in its destruction. Briefly summarize God's grievances or woes against Babylon in the verses below.[57] Which of these grievances could God have against our culture?

2:6-8   _____

2:9-11   _____

2:12-14 _____

2:15-17 _____

2:18-20 _____

5. God's Witnesses

In 2:11, God says "the stone will cry out from the wall." Even stones will be witnesses against the Babylonians who occupy or build with stolen property.

a) Read Luke 19:37-40. Jesus quotes Habakkuk during His triumphal entry into Jerusalem on Palm Sunday. Jesus was riding a colt among a large crowd of followers who loudly praised God for the miracles they had seen Jesus perform. The religious leaders hated hearing people praise Jesus and did not want the exuberant crowd to get out of control. What did the Pharisees demand? What do you think Jesus' response to the Pharisees' criticism meant?

b) Injustice is never hidden from God's eyes. When people are persecuted or silenced, Creation is still a witness to the injustice. Metaphorically speaking, the very stones of the buildings will cry out to God for justice. How can this realization comfort those who feel oppressed and alone?

c) Read Joshua 24:24-27. Long before Habakkuk, Joshua held a covenant renewal ceremony after leading the Israelites into the Promised Land. The people promised to obey the Lord. What would serve as a witness against the Israelites if they violated the covenant?

6. God's Glory

In v. 13-14, God says the Babylonians' efforts at empire building are in vain because the results will eventually be consumed. Even King Nebuchadnezzar's vast, exploitative building programs achieved only momentary, limited glory. The king's temporary glory in Babylon contrasts with the Lord's everlasting glory which covers the whole world.

a) The classic Babylonian myth, *Epic of Gilgamesh,* contains legends about an ancient king named Gilgamesh who wanted to attain immortality.[58]

Gilgamesh eventually concluded that the only immortality for humans was through lasting works of civilization and culture. Why does his conclusion miss the mark?

b) In v. 14, God quotes a messianic passage from Isaiah. Just as God used Assyria to punish Israel in Isaiah's day, God will use Babylon to punish Judah in Habakkuk's day. After punishment there will be glorious restoration of all creation through the Messiah. The restoration has already begun with Christ's first coming, continues through His church today, and will be fulfilled at His second coming. Write in the space below what Isaiah foretold will be the result of God's restoration (see Isaiah 11:9b).

c) In v. 14, God also quotes the book of Numbers, recalling that the Israelites who had been privileged to see God's glory refused to enter the Promised Land. God punished their contempt and disobedience with forty years of wandering in the wilderness. Write in the space below what God said will happen someday with regard to His glory (see Numbers 14:21).

d) Notice that the above passages from Isaiah and Numbers are combined in Habakkuk: "For the earth will be filled with the knowledge of the glory of the LORD as the waters cover the sea." All people will have knowledge of God; more specifically, they will know His glory, meaning His radiant, powerful presence throughout the world. What recent incident in the news makes you long for the world to know God's glory in this way? While you wait for the eschatological (end times) fulfillment of Scripture's vision, how will you reflect God's glory now?

Part III: Personal Application and Growth

Today's lesson points to several important truths that apply to our personal lives. Allow these truths to penetrate your mind, soften your heart, deepen your faith and affect your behavior to help you continually grow in Christ.

1. We are to trust that God is good, powerful, and just, and has a morally sufficient reason for allowing evil to exist in the world.

The presence of evil and suffering in the world should not be a hindrance to belief in God. As mentioned in this lesson, people can only speak meaningfully of evil if God exists. Also, pain and suffering may at times serve a good purpose such as with medical treatment. How will you answer someone who rejects God because of evil and suffering in the world?

2. The righteous will live by faith in Christ's saving work.

Read this truth by putting emphasis on the word *righteous;* then read it with emphasis on *live;* then *faith*. Which emphasis means the most to you personally? Why? How will it impact your life this week to remember that the righteous will live by faith in Christ?

3. Our lives are to honor and reflect the splendor of God's radiant glory.

There is something different about people who spend a lot of time with God. There is a spiritual brightness about them, a reflection of God's radiant glory. How will you adjust your schedule to regularly spend more time with God? As you spend time with God and reflect His glory more and more, what areas of your life will become spiritually brighter?

Part IV: Closing Prayer

by John Calvin

Grant, Almighty God, that as the corruption of our flesh ever leads us to pride and vain confidence, we may be illuminated by your word so as to understand how great and how grievous is our poverty, and be thus taught wholly to deny ourselves;

And so to present ourselves exposed before you, that we may not hope for righteousness or for salvation from any other source than from your mercy alone, nor seek any rest but only in Christ;

And may we cleave to you by the sacred and inviolable bond of faith, that we may boldly despise all those empty boastings by which the ungodly exult over us, and that we may also so cast ourselves down in true humility that thereby we may be carried upward above all heavens and become partakers of that eternal life which your only begotten Son has purchased for us by His own blood. Amen.[59]

❧ Lesson 12 ❧
Habakkuk's Prayer of Faith
Habakkuk 3:1-19

Part I: Setting the Stage

Purpose

The final lesson of our study brings us to Habakkuk's beautiful prayer of trust and joy. Habakkuk's closing prayer shows that he has come a long way from the opening verses of his book. Despite the coming Babylonian destruction he has moved from asking "Why?" and "How long?" to offering praise. The important lesson of Habakkuk lies here. Whether or not we understand or like what God is doing, we are to respond in faith and joyful worship.

Look for the following application points in this lesson:

1. Man's primary purpose is to glorify God and to enjoy Him forever.
2. The best way for God's people to remain faithful is to remember who God is and what He has done in Jesus Christ.
3. If you are frustrated with God's mysterious ways, turn your frustration into trust and joy by submitting your will to God's will, no matter what the circumstances.

Job's Praise

When people read Habakkuk's complaints they are often reminded of Job, a righteous man who suffered great sorrow and loss. Job's suffering did not seem fair and he struggled to understand why God allowed it. Like Habakkuk, Job did not doubt God's character. He complained because he could not make sense out of his terrible suffering in light of God's goodness, power, sovereignty, and justice. Although God answered Job, Job never got the explanations he wanted. In the end Job realized the only appropriate response to the trials of life was to humbly and faithfully trust God (Job 42:1-6).

Abraham's Trust

Abraham is another Old Testament figure who demonstrated faith even when God's ways did not make sense. When God first called Abraham (Abram) to be in covenant relationship with Him, God promised to give Abraham land, descendants, and to make him a blessing to the nations. As the years passed and no children were born to Abraham and his wife Sarah, Abraham complained to God about God's failure to fulfill the covenant promise of descendants. Abraham's complaint rose out of his strong faith that the Lord was able to do anything He pleased.

God answered Abraham's complaint by repeating His covenant promises. Abraham did not get the explanations he sought at the time but he put his trust in God and believed Him (Genesis 15:2-6). Because of his faith Abraham became an heir to God's righteousness. In fact, the New Testament considers Abraham to be the spiritual father of everyone who believes God (Romans 4:11-12).

Habakkuk's Faith

In spite of his complaints about what God was doing, Habakkuk comes to the conclusion, "Yet I will rejoice in the LORD, I will take joy in the God of my salvation" (Habakkuk 3:18). Without knowing the details of how God will save, Habakkuk joyfully puts his faith in God his Lord and Savior.

Our Joy

All of us have times in our faith journey when we echo Habakkuk's initial frustration. Perhaps God does not seem to hear our cries, or He tells us to be patient with the current awful situation, or He reveals a solution so terrible we can hardly believe it. These times are a test of our faith, for God wants us to trust that He is always working for our good. He wants us to arrive at the same conclusion as Habakkuk, allowing our questions and worries to turn into worship.

We have the privilege of knowing God's ultimate plan of salvation in Jesus Christ. Our happiness is not based on outward circumstances, material blessings, or freedom from trials, but on Christ's redeeming work which restores our relationship with God. We therefore have an inner joy that overflows in praise to God. This is what all of humanity was created for. The 17th century *Westminster Shorter Catechism* rightly affirms, "Man's primary purpose is to glorify God and to enjoy Him forever."[60]

Part II: Studying Scripture

Read Habakkuk 3:1-7

Habakkuk's prayer is a song in the style of the psalms, much like the style of Jonah's prayer of thanksgiving. The words *shigionoth* at the beginning and *selah* in the body are features found in many psalms, perhaps indicating some sort of musical notation or instruction. The postscript at the very end of Habakkuk's psalm mentions the director of music and stringed instruments, confirming that it was designed to be set to music.

1. Remember

The psalm opens with an invocation calling on God to display His wrath against His enemies. Habakkuk longs for justice. At the same time, Habakkuk knows that God's fearsome retribution against His enemies will affect God's people. There will be collateral damage.

a) In v. 2, what does Habakkuk ask God to remember concerning His people?

b) At the same time, what does God want His people to remember concerning Him? (See Judges 2:1)

c) Habakkuk asks God to renew His past saving acts and he also speaks about God's merciful character. Remembering what God has done (His savings acts) and who He is (His character) are the main ways for God's people to stay faithful to Him. What aspects of God's saving acts and character do you enjoy reflecting on?

2. God the Victorious One

God sends a vision which Habakkuk records in three stanzas. Habakkuk uses poetic language to describe God's past victories over the Egyptians and Canaanites. In the first stanza (v. 3-7) Habakkuk portrays the powerful covenant God marching along as He leads Israel from Mount Sinai during the Exodus. Habakkuk employs anthropomorphic language, meaning that he describes God as having human characteristics like hands and feet for literary effect.

a) In v. 5, what curses fell on God's enemies?

b) In v. 6-7, how invincible are the nations and nature compared to God?

Read Habakkuk 3:8-15

3. God the Divine Warrior

In the second stanza (v. 8-11) and the third stanza (v. 12-15) Habakkuk uses the image of a thunderstorm to describe the approach of God, the divine warrior. The divine warrior concept was closely connected to the idea of covenant, the Exodus, and the conquest of Canaan. God would vanquish His enemies to save His chosen people. He had done it in the past, and Habakkuk is confident He will do it again.

a) God riding on His horses in v. 8 and 15 forms an *inclusio* or enclosure around the second and third stanzas. Metaphorically, God rides storm clouds victoriously into battle on behalf of His people. The rumble of horses and chariots represent thunder. In v. 9 and 11, how is lightning described?

b) Babylonian warfare (1:8-11) is nothing compared to that of God the divine warrior (3:8-15). Point out a few things that show God's superiority.

c) Like Jonah's song, Habakkuk's song includes references to about a dozen psalms. Habakkuk relies particularly on Psalm 18 for storm imagery describing how God the divine warrior rescues His people. See how many action verbs you can find in Psalm 18:9-14 and Habakkuk 3:8-15 that show God's extensive effort and activity in saving His people.

4. God's Anointed One

In v. 13, various interpretations have been offered for the "anointed." The term could mean God's people in general or the Davidic line in particular (God went forth for the salvation *of* His anointed.) It could also mean Christ or an earthly king went with God (God went forth for salvation *with* His anointed.)

The Hebrew word for "anointed one" is *masiah* (messiah) and it is only used in one other place in the prophets. Isaiah speaks of Cyrus as God's anointed one who will subdue nations (Isaiah 45:1). It is possible that Habakkuk expects God to raise up this unknown Cyrus to defeat Babylon someday like Isaiah predicted. That prediction came true when Cyrus, king of Persia, defeated Babylon and allowed the Jewish exiles to return to Judah. It is also possible that on a more profound level Habakkuk expects a Messiah beyond Cyrus, just as Isaiah expected a messianic Suffering Servant in addition to Cyrus. Whichever way we interpret the verse, Jesus Christ is the ultimate fulfillment of all messianic hope.

a)   In v. 13, who is contrasted with the anointed one?

b)   How does it make you feel to know that the Lord who controls all the forces of nature and history cares about His people and takes action to save them?

Read Habakkuk 3:16-19

5. Habakkuk's Faith in God

In this passage Habakkuk gives us one of the most profound and memorable expressions of faith in the Bible. While God sends the Babylonians to punish His people's sin, Habakkuk will patiently wait for God to turn His wrath on the invaders and end His people's punishment. Habakkuk no longer questions God.

a)   The opening and closing stanzas of Habakkuk's prayer are autobiographical. "I have heard" (3:2) and "I hear" (3:16) form an *inclusio* or enclosure around the three stanzas. In v. 16, how does Habakkuk respond to God's revelation?

b)   The prophet Isaiah earlier had a vision in which he was overwhelmed by God's holiness. Isaiah said he was "lost" or "ruined," literally "cut off" (Isaiah 6:5). When have you experienced God's holiness or power during worship or another time in such a way that you felt physically undone? What was it like?

c)   What is Habakkuk's attitude now about the timing of God's justice? How will his example help you face problems and trials that seem to have no end?

d) In v. 17-18, the loss of fruit, wine, oil, vegetables, grain and livestock due to the ravages of war are a description of devastating hunger and poverty. Despite the expected loss of essential material blessings of food, shelter, and clothing, Habakkuk goes on to express confidence in God his Savior. The Puritan Matthew Henry comments on this passage,

> "When all is gone his God is not gone... Those who, when they were full, *enjoyed God in all*, when they are emptied and impoverished can *enjoy all in God*, and can sit down upon a melancholy heap of the ruins of all their creature comforts and even then can sing to the praise and glory of God, as the God of their salvation. This is the principal ground of our joy in God."[61]

What will you do now to make it more likely you will continue to praise God if you suffer severe material losses in the future?

e) In v. 19, in the face of uncertainty Habakkuk confidently declares that God is his strength and stability. He quotes Psalm 18:33, "He made my feet like the feet of a deer and set me secure on the heights." What an amazing faith journey we have been privileged to witness:

Frustration (1:2-4) → Submission (2:1) → Trust and Joy (3:17-19)

Looking at this progression, what is the key to Habakkuk's movement from worry to worship; fear to faith; complaint to praise; low places to high places? What have you learned from Habakkuk about ending up with an attitude of trust and joy when you experience frustration over God's ways?

6. Habakkuk, Jonah, and Us

As this study comes to a close, take a moment to think about the similarities between the prophets Jonah and Habakkuk. Both of them knew that God was holy, righteous, powerful, loving, and faithful. They both wanted God to punish sin and demonstrate divine justice. When they did not see evidence of God's judgment against the wicked they took their complaints directly to God, and their cranky demands were honest and direct.

But that is where the similarities end. When God answered their complaints in ways they did not like, they responded in opposite manners. At the end of his book Jonah remained arrogant, defiant, rebellious, and angry at God. His outward obedience was reluctant and resentful. He refused to acknowledge God's sovereignty and would not align his will with God's. Habakkuk, on the other hand, finally came to a place of complete submission to God's will. He acknowledged God's sovereign right to run the world and he offered heartfelt, joyful praise to God no matter what.

a) Clearly we are to imitate Habakkuk's faith in contrast to the example Jonah gives us. What specific steps will you take to imitate Habakkuk when you don't like what God is doing or you can't make sense of it?

b) Take a moment to look at the application points at the end of each lesson (see the complete list in Appendix A). Which are most important to you? Why? How will you continue to use these points to remind you of what you have learned from your study of Jonah and Habakkuk?

c) Both Jonah and Habakkuk allow us to witness their passionate struggle with God over issues of good and evil, justice and mercy, sovereignty and grace. Their honest conversations with God encourage us to come to God with our concerns, but also with respectful, repentant hearts. How will you find a trusted group of Christian friends who can pray with you and hold you accountable when you go through spiritual struggles with God?

d) Ask the Holy Spirit to continue to apply God's word to your heart and mind so that the insights you have gained will be a lasting blessing to you and others.

Part III: Personal Application and Growth

Today's lesson points to several important truths that apply to our personal lives. Allow these truths to penetrate your mind, soften your heart, deepen your faith and affect your behavior to help you continually grow in Christ.

1. Man's primary purpose is to glorify God and to enjoy Him forever.

We were made for a purpose. We fulfill the purpose for which we were made when we glorify God through Jesus Christ and thereby enjoy Him in this lifetime and into eternity. What are some of the ways you will glorify God this week? Describe which aspects of your life (physical, emotional, spiritual, relational) will be changed the most by your abiding sense of joy.

2. The best way for God's people to remain faithful is to remember who God is and what He has done in Jesus Christ.

What specific events and characteristics of God do you plan to think of when you become discouraged or sluggish in your faith? Why will remembering Jesus Christ strengthen your faith and help you respond to trials with faith?

3. If you are frustrated with God's mysterious ways, turn your frustration into trust and joy by submitting your will to God's will, no matter what the circumstances.

Habakkuk models the right way and Jonah shows the wrong way for us to respond to God when we are frustrated with God or don't like what He is doing. What are the most important changes you will make in the way you respond to God?

Part IV: Closing Prayer

by John Calvin

Grant, Almighty God, that as we have a continual contest with powerful enemies, we may know that we are defended by your hand and that you are fighting for us when we are at rest, so that we may boldly contend under your protection and never be wearied, nor yield to Satan and the wicked, or to any temptations, but firmly proceed in the course of our warfare;

And however much you may often humble us, so as to make us tremble under your awful judgment, may we yet never cease to entertain firm hope, since you have once promised to be to us an eternal Father in your eternal and only begotten Son;

But being confirmed by the invincible constancy of faith, may we so submit ourselves to you as to bear all our afflictions patiently till you gather us at length into that blessed rest which has been procured for us by the blood of your own Son. Amen.[62]

❧ Appendix A ❧
Application Points

A list of the personal application points at the end of each lesson.

SECTION I: THE PROPHET JONAH

Lesson 1 The Role of Old Testament Prophets
God revealed His redemptive purposes through His representatives, the Old Testament prophets, and ultimately through Jesus Christ.
Some prophecies were conditional and others were unconditional.
God continues to speak to us today through the writings of the prophets.

Lesson 2 Introducing Jonah
God uses unexpected methods and people to further His plans of salvation.
Prosperity alone cannot solve social problems because there are underlying spiritual issues.
We must continue to obey God's word and His call on our lives rather than coasting on our reputation of past obedience.

Lesson 3 Jonah's Disobedience
Our obedience to God should be immediate and active.
We are never out of God's sight, nor can we thwart His purposes.
God guides us by His written word and sometimes by circumstances, but we should never be guided by circumstances that conflict with His word.

Lesson 4 The Grace of God
Our laments should end in praise to God.
Learning the psalms and their context can be a source of strength and comfort in difficult times.

Repentance involves gratitude for Christ's saving work and a commitment to live obediently under His lordship.

Lesson 5 Jonah's Evangelism
There are about seven billion people in the world and every single one of them is important to God no matter where they live.
God wants to use your personal testimony and abilities for evangelism purposes.
We are forgiven in Christ and so in gratitude we are to forgive others.

Lesson 6 Jonah's Cranky Prayer
God is gracious, merciful, slow to anger, abounding in love, and relenting from disaster.
We should praise God for generously providing unearned blessings to us.
Christians are to be excellent goers or senders with a heart for missions.

Lesson 7 The Sovereignty of God
We need to align our will with God's, particularly in the areas of obedience to His word, mercy to others, and submission to His sovereignty.
Choose life by loving God, obeying His word, and holding fast to Him.
Lift your eyes to the bigger picture and learn to see the world from God's point of view.

Lesson 8 Jesus and the Sign of Jonah
God is in control of the world and runs it every second of every day by His providence.
The kingdom of God has come into the world, but consummation of the kingdom is still to come.
There is no need to demand more proof of who Jesus is, for we have all the evidence we need recorded in Scripture.

SECTION II: THE PROPHET HABAKKUK

Lesson 9 Habakkuk's First Complaint
God wants us to speak to Him candidly, boldly, and respectfully.
Faithful waiting for God's justice is active waiting:
> Trust in God's unfailing love
> Rejoice in God's salvation

Sing of God's goodness
Look at the bigger picture
Be astounded at what God is doing
Believe God's word

We should prepare ourselves spiritually in good times so we can face unexpected problems.

Lesson 10 Habakkuk's Second Complaint
God is the great I AM, the Creator, the Holy One of Israel, and our Rock.
Even in the darkest hours of history God saves a remnant of true believers, because His church, Christ's body, will always be present in the world.
We can wait patiently and confidently for God's justice, trusting His perfect ways.

Lesson 11 The Justice of God
We are to trust that God is good, powerful, and just, and has a morally sufficient reason for allowing evil to exist in the world.
The righteous will live by faith in Christ's saving work.
Our lives are to honor and reflect the splendor of God's radiant glory.

Lesson 12 Habakkuk's Prayer of Faith
Man's primary purpose is to glorify God and to enjoy Him forever.
The best way for God's people to remain faithful is to remember who God is and what He has done in Jesus Christ.
If you are frustrated with God's mysterious ways, turn your frustration into trust and joy by submitting your will to God's will, no matter what the circumstances.

❧ Appendix B ☙
Leader's Guide

This leader's guide is intended to help you get the most out of your group study of *God's Cranky Prophets: Jonah & Habakkuk*. Whether one person leads all the lessons or the leadership is passed around, it is hoped that this guide will encourage and equip the leader to present the lessons in a way that meets the needs of individuals and the group as a whole.

The Goal of Bible Study
The overall goal of Bible study is for lives to be transformed through the power of God's word applied by the Holy Spirit. Studying Scripture should change one's mind, heart and behavior for Christ. Encourage participants to engage their emotions and cognitive thinking as they study, and put the truths of Scripture into practice in their personal lives.

Overall Planning
There are 12 lessons in this study. Each lesson is designed to take about an hour for group discussion, plus you will want to provide additional time for announcements, prayer concerns, and fellowship. You should feel free to make adjustments to cover the material in a way that fits your group's particular schedule and interest.

Homework for Participants
Everyone will get more out of the Scripture and lessons if they answer the study questions ahead of time, including the first lesson. Encourage participants to set aside time to do the homework. Thoughtful preparation will allow participants to follow the group discussion better, and they will be more ready for deeper levels of insight.

The reality, of course, is that most people are pressed for time. Not everyone will be able to fully prepare ahead of time. By all means be gracious to them. They will be blessed by participating in the group even if it is the first time they have read the material.

Leader Preparation

The leader should do the same homework as the participants. In addition, there are a couple of things the leader will want to do to be better prepared:

1. Pray for participants by name during the week. Lift up their individual concerns to the Lord and pray that each person will find time to study.
2. Glance at the Endnotes to see if there is additional background information for the lesson that will be helpful.

Appreciating Differences

A good leader will remember that people approach a Bible study text with different expectations influenced by their style of learning:[63]

- Imaginative learners want to see the big picture and know why the information is important before they get started.
- Analytic learners like lots of facts and details and enjoy learning information for its own sake.
- Common sense learners solve problems and want to put the information to practical use.
- Dynamic learners are creative and want to find ways to apply the information in their personal life.

Keep in mind that people also have different learning modes. Your preferred mode may or may not match others in the group. For instance, visual learners tend to like maps and auditory learners may appreciate poetry.

People take part in Bible study groups for a number of valid reasons. Some people hunger to know God's word more deeply or need a safe place to ask hard spiritual questions, while others long for comforting fellowship and intercessory prayer. Some may just be curious.

Ask the Lord to help you be compassionate and sensitive to the wide range of learning styles, modes, motivations, and needs among your group.

Leading the Lesson

Start with a prayer asking the Holy Spirit to enlighten your hearts and minds with the truth of Scripture and apply it to your lives.

Part I: Setting the Stage

Read the opening pages out loud. These remarks tell what the lesson is about, why it is important, and relevant background material. Imaginative learners will benefit from knowing the big picture of the lesson up front.

Part II: Studying Scripture

Ask a volunteer to read the Scripture passage out loud. Do not press someone to read in front of others if they are not comfortable. Be kind and supportive if someone gets a passage with names that are difficult to pronounce.

Read each study question out loud and invite answers. Most of your time will be spent on these questions. The leader should not be the first to answer the study questions and should not even add further comments if the group's answers are sufficient. Watch the time and try not to let anyone dominate the discussion. Analytic learners will especially enjoy this part of the lesson with its emphasis on facts and interpretation of Scripture.

Part III: Personal Application and Growth

Read each application point out loud and invite answers to the questions. If a point is too personal, allow people to reflect silently on their commitment to change. Ask if anyone wants to offer additional points of application.

Dynamic and common sense learners will welcome the chance to apply the lesson in practical ways in the coming week. All learning styles will benefit from questions that challenge them to envision the way their faith will mature as a result of applying the lesson.

Part IV: Closing Prayer

Read Calvin's prayer out loud and close with a brief prayer of your own.

❧ Appendix C ❧
About Hermeneutics

"Then we will no longer be infants, tossed back and forth by the waves,
and blown here and there by every wind of teaching..."
(Ephesians 4:14)

Certain principles guide our study of the Bible so that we remain faithful to the Biblical text. We do not want to get lost in unfounded speculation. It is considered good procedure when police detectives follow established guidelines during investigations so they do not overlook evidence or draw wrong conclusions. Similarly, we will follow established guidelines for Bible study. These guidelines belong to the field of hermeneutics (her-men-OO-ticks).

Everyone studies the Bible with a hermeneutic, a set of interpretive principles. Even people who have never heard of the word can appreciate that the way they interpret a passage is influenced by their understanding of history, grammar, and logic. One thing that can make Bible study perplexing, though, is that there is no definitive hermeneutic with which everyone agrees. That means different scholars might come up with different interpretations of a passage depending on which interpretive principles they apply.

The choice of interpretive principles is extremely important since a faulty hermeneutic can lead even well-meaning people to misguided conclusions. Evangelical scholars generally adhere to certain traditional rules of interpretation based on Reformation principles covering four areas: historical, cultural, theological, and literary. This is the grammatico-historical approach. It is designed to discover the author's original intended meaning by looking at the background, context, theology, and grammatical features.

The following list gives a few of the principles this study is based on. A good study Bible like *The Reformation Study Bible (ESV)* can provide some of the background, language analysis, and commentary suggested below.

Seven Principles of Interpretation

1. Consider the historical setting.
Study the period of history in which the incident occurred or was recorded. Learn about the rulers of the day, natural disasters, and major events. For example, look at New Testament events in the context of the Roman Empire.

2. Study the cultural setting.
Learn about the customs, food, clothing, religion, geography, and economics of the time. Consider the national and racial backgrounds of the people involved.

3. Read the Scriptural context.
Read the immediate context consisting of the paragraph and chapter in which the verse is located. Then look at the broader context of the whole book, other books by the same author, and the entire Bible.

4. Appreciate the unity of the Old and New Testaments.
When reading a New Testament text, discover whether it alludes to the Old Testament and what its connection teaches us. When reading the Old Testament, ask what the passage teaches about God's redemptive purposes which are ultimately fulfilled in Jesus Christ.

5. Let Scripture interpret Scripture ("the analogy of faith").
Interpret a difficult passage in light of related, clear passages. Read the clear passages first and then read the difficult one in light of their meaning.

6. Read the Bible in a literary way (*sensus literalis*).
Identify the literary genre of the passage (poetry, narrative, letter, etc.) Look for metaphors and literary structure. Remember that poetry, prophecy, and apocalyptic are not meant to be read in a consistently literal way.

7. Go back to the original languages (*ad fontes*, "to the source").
Study a translation of the Bible rather than a paraphrased version. The Old Testament was written mostly in Hebrew and the New Testament in Greek.

❧ Select Bibliography ❧

Apologetics
Bahnsen, Greg L. *Always Ready*. Nacogdoches, TX: Covenant Media Press, 1996.

Keller, Timothy. *The Reason for God: Belief in an Age of Skepticism*. New York: Dutton, 2008.

Packer, J. I. *Knowing God*. Downers Grove, IL: InterVarsity Press, 1973.

Pearcey, Nancy. *Total Truth: Liberating Christianity from Its Cultural Captivity*. Wheaton, IL: Crossway Books, 2005.

_____. *Saving Leonardo: A Call to Resist the Secular Assault on Mind, Morals, & Meaning*. Nashville: B & H Publishing Group, 2010.

Schaefer, Francis A. *The God Who Is There*. Downers Grove, IL: InterVarsity Press, 1982.

Sproul, R. C. *Defending Your Faith: An Introduction to Apologetics*. Wheaton, IL: Crossway Books, 2003; http://www.ligonier.org/store.

Strobel, Lee. *The Case for Christ: A Journalist's Personal Investigation of the Evidence for Jesus*. Grand Rapids, MI: Zondervan, 1998.

Calling and Missions
Elliot, Elisabeth. *God's Guidance: Finding His Will for Your Life*. Grand Rapids, MI: Revell, 1997.

Piper, John. *Let the Nations Be Glad*. Grand Rapids, MI: Baker Academic, 2003.

Wilson, Josh. "I Refuse," Music video. *See You*, 2011; http://www. joshwilsonmusic.com/audio.

Commentaries
Baker, David W., T. Desmond Alexander and Bruce Waltke. *Obadiah, Jonah, Micah*. The Tyndale Old Testament Commentaries. Downers Grove, IL: Inter-Varsity Press, 1988.

Robertson, O. Palmer. *The Books of Nahum, Habakkuk, and Zephaniah*. The New International Commentary on the Old Testament (NICOT). Grand Rapids, MI: William B. Eerdmans Publishing Company, 1990.

Stuart, Douglas. *Word Biblical Commentary: Hosea-Jonah*. Vol. 31. Nashville: Thomas Nelson, 1987.

Leading a Bible Study
Bennett, Dennis. "How We Teach and How They Learn." *Equip to Disciple*. Series of ten articles. Lawrenceville, GA: Presbyterian Church in America, 2009-2011; http://www.pcacdm.org/archives.

Nielson, Kathleen Buswell. *Bible Study: Following the Ways of the Word*. Phillipsburg, NJ: P & R Publishing Company, 2011.

Reference Books
Arnold, Bill T. and Bryan E. Beyer. *Encountering the Old Testament: A Christian Survey*. 2nd Ed. Grand Rapids, MI: Baker Academic, 2008.

Frame, John M. *The Doctrine of God*. Phillipsburg, NJ: P & R Publishing, 2002.

Grudem, Wayne. *Systematic Theology: An Introduction to Biblical Doctrine*. Grand Rapids, MI: Zondervan, 1994.

Waiting
Carson, D. A. *How Long, O Lord?* Grand Rapids, MI: BakerBooks, 1990.

❧ Endnotes ❦

Introduction

[1]   Robert L. Reymond, *A New Systematic Theology of the Christian Faith* (Nashville, TN: Thomas Nelson Publishers, 1998), 377.

Lesson 1: The Role of Old Testament Prophets

[2]   PART I: Setting the Stage, "Other Prophets"
Some of the prophets listed may not be familiar to you:
Huldah was a prophetess who counseled good King Josiah (II Kings 22:14-20).
Nathan confronted King David after his sin with Bathsheba (II Sam. 12:1-15).
Shemaiah advised King Rehoboam, Solomon's son (I Kings 12:21-24).
Micaiah opposed wicked King Ahab (I Kings 22:6-8).

[3]   Charles H. Spurgeon, "Jesus Near But Unrecognized," *Spurgeon's Sermons*, Vol. 20, No. 1180 (1874); http://www.ccel.org/search/fulltext/Spurgeon%20 Emmaus; Public Domain.

[4]   PART II: Studying Scripture, Question 5d, "Continuity"
John the Baptist calls Jesus two important titles that imply He is our Lord and Savior.
"Lamb of God" points to Jesus' humanity and blood sacrifice; our Savior (Jn. 1:29).
"Son of God" points to Jesus' divinity; our Lord (Jn. 1:34).

[5]   John Calvin, *Commentary on Hosea*, Lecture 9: Hosea; http://www.ccel.org/c/ calvin; Public Domain.

Lesson 2: Introducing Jonah

[6]   PART I: Setting the Stage, "A Faithful Prophet"
Jesus mentions a martyr named Zechariah, probably not the minor prophet since the minor prophet Zechariah is not known to have been martyred. Abel and the martyr Zechariah are the first and last martyrs in the Hebrew Bible and represent all righteous martyrs from A to Z, so to speak (Matt. 23:35).

[7]   PART II: Studying Scripture, Question 1b, "Jonah's Background"
Jeroboam I started as an official in King Solomon's court (I Kings 12). Jeroboam led a rebellion against Solomon but fled to Egypt for safety. When Solomon died, Jeroboam returned to Israel to lead the northern tribes in rebellion against Solomon's son, Rehoboam. The kingdom divided and Jeroboam reigned as first king of the northern kingdom of Israel; Rehoboam reigned in the southern kingdom of Judah. Jeroboam set up worship centers at Bethel and Dan in the north to rival Jerusalem in Judah. There were several evil aspects to Jeroboam's actions:

He led people away from Jerusalem, God's ordained central place of worship.
He introduced idolatrous worship of golden calves.
He built shrines on Canaanite religious high places that should have been destroyed.
He appointed a non-Levite priesthood in defiance of Mosaic Law.
He created a religious feast day not sanctioned by God.

[8]   Sinclair B. Ferguson, *Man Overboard! The Story of Jonah* (Edinburgh: Banner of Truth Trust, 2008), 8; www.banneroftruth.co.uk.

[9]   John Calvin, *Commentary on Jonah, Micah, Nahum,* Lecture 72: Jonah; http://www.ccel.org/c/calvin; Public Domain.

Lesson 3: Jonah's Disobedience

[10]   Elisabeth Elliot, *God's Guidance: Finding His Will for Your Life* (Grand Rapids, MI: Revell, 1997), 19-20.

[11]   PART II: Studying Scripture, Question 3b, "Fleeing from God"
Psalm 139:7-10 refers to virtually all the directions we can possibly go:
Up: Represented by heaven or the heavens, away from the earth.
Down: Represented by Sheol (land of the dead), into the depths of the earth.
East: Represented by morning or dawn.
West: Represented by the far side or uttermost parts of the Mediterranean Sea.

[12]   J. I. Packer, *Knowing God* (Downers Grove, IL: InterVarsity Press, 1973), 239.

[13]   Sinclair B. Ferguson, *Man Overboard! The Story of Jonah,* 22-23.

[14]   John Calvin, *Commentary on Jonah, Micah, Nahum,* Lecture 75: Jonah.

Lesson 4: The Grace of God

[15] David W. Baker, T. Desmond Alexander and Bruce Waltke, *Obadiah, Jonah, Micah*, Tyndale Old Testament Commentaries (Downers Grove, IL: Inter-Varsity Press, 1988), 110-111.

PART I: Setting the Stage, "A Miracle"
One such incident apparently occurred in 1891 when a whaler named James Bartley was swallowed by a large sperm whale in the south Atlantic while Bartley was trying to harpoon it. The whale was later killed and Bartley was found unconscious but alive in its stomach. The story's validity is uncertain, because years after the incident the ship captain's widow is said to have denied that it ever happened.

[16] John Calvin, *Commentary on Jonah, Micah, Nahum*, Lecture 76: Jonah.

[17] PART II: Studying Scripture, Question 4a, "Down, Down, Down and Up"
Repetition of a term or a theme three times is a literary technique to add emphasis:
Great: Great city (1:2); great wind (1:4); great fish (1:17).
Fear: Fear of a storm (1:5); of God the Creator (1:10); of God the Ruler (1:16).
Down: Down to Joppa (1:3); down into the ship (1:5); down into the sea (2:6).
Death: Preferable to God's call (1:12); to God's mercy (4:3); to God's sovereignty (4:9).

[18] Mark D. Futato, *Basic Hebrew* (BibleWorks, LLC; CDROM 2005; 2003), Lesson 9.

[19] PART II: Studying Scripture, Question 6, "Our Lord and Savior"
Some Christians wrongly teach that we can accept Jesus as Savior without accepting Him as Lord. They derogatorily call the orthodox view of Jesus as Lord and Savior "lordship salvation." However, Scripture solidly supports the teaching that Jesus is both our Savior and Lord. Our acceptance of His salvation is incomplete unless we also accept Him as Lord of our lives.

[20] John Calvin, *Commentary on Jonah, Micah, Nahum*, Lecture 76: Jonah.

Lesson 5: Jonah's Evangelism

[21] Douglas Stuart, *Word Biblical Commentary: Hosea-Jonah*, Vol. 31 (Nashville, TN: Thomas Nelson, 1987), 491-2.

PART I: Setting the Stage, "A City Prepared By God"
First ominous event: There was a total solar eclipse when a new moon passed between the sun and earth on June 15, 763/762 B.C. at 8:00 in the morning. It lasted five minutes and was visible in Cyprus, Syria, and northern Assyria within a few miles of Nineveh. This eclipse is mentioned in Assyrian records and is the oldest verified solar eclipse ever recorded. It would have been accompanied by unusual physical effects besides darkness: variations in gravity and the atmosphere; visibility of Mercury, certain stars, and the sun's corona; and different shadow patterns on the ground.

Fourth ominous event: There were periodic invasions by the Urartians north of Assyria. Urartu (Armenia) was one of the most powerful kingdoms in the ancient near east. At this point in history its army was at its peak and reached into Assyria as far south as Babylon. The Assyrians were unable to control the Urartians until the rise of the Assyrian king Tiglath-Pileser III in 745 B.C., after Jonah's time.

[22]   J. Edwin Orr, *The Second Evangelical Awakening* (London: Marshall Morgan and Scott, 1964), 48-49; referenced by Sinclair B. Ferguson, *Man Overboard! The Story of Jonah,* 65-66.

[23]   David W. Baker, et al., *Obadiah, Jonah, Micah,* 56.

PART II: Studying Scripture, Question 3, "Evangelism in the City"
Archaeologists have uncovered two mounds on which the city of ancient Nineveh was built. One mound is known as *Navi Yunus* (Prophet Jonah), a reminder of Jonah's impact on the city. Excavations of ancient Nineveh have been discontinued.

[24]   Jonathan Edwards, "Sinners in the Hands of an Angry God;" http://www.ccel. org/edwards/sermons.sinners.html; Public Domain.

[25]   John Calvin, *Commentary on Jonah, Micah, Nahum,* Lecture 77: Jonah.

Lesson 6: Jonah's Cranky Prayer
[26]   *Westminster Shorter Catechism,* Question 4; http://www.ccel.org/ccel/ anonymous/westminster; Public Domain.

[27]   PART I: Setting the Stage, "God's Attributes"
Systematic theology organizes religious truths of the Bible into coherent categories of theological thought. Typically, a systematic theology includes:
Doctrine of God (His Being, word, attributes, Trinity; His work of Creation)
Doctrine of Man (the image of God; sin)

Doctrine of Christ and the Holy Spirit (the person and work of Christ; the Holy Spirit)

Doctrine of Redemption Applied (faith; justification; sanctification; perseverance)

Doctrine of the Church and Sacraments

Doctrine of the End Times (eschatology; death; heaven; hell; Christ's return)

[28]   PART II: Studying Scripture, Question 1c, "Jonah's Anger"

Commentators offer various reasons for Jonah's anger:

Nationalism: The view that Jonah resented helping Israel's enemy Assyria is commonly held by those who assume the book was written by a later author who looked back on the destruction of Israel by Assyria and attributed intense anger over the event to Jonah. Others, however, see the book's description of Nineveh's weak king as evidence that the book was written before Assyria became a global power that destroyed Israel.

Ethnocentrism: Some suggest that Jonah was jealous that God could care for Gentiles (non-Jews). Others point out, though, that Jonah was willing to die so God would save the Gentile sailors during the storm.

Theodicy: Jonah's anger was evidently related to his frustration over the way God dealt with the wicked. It infuriated Jonah that God would save wicked Nineveh. Later he was enraged that God would destroy an innocent plant. Jonah's refusal to accept God's sovereignty in matters of salvation, justice, and mercy led him to despair.

[29]   Timothy Keller, *The Prodigal God* (New York: Dutton, 2008), 49.

[30]   John Piper, *Let the Nations Be Glad* (Grand Rapids, MI: Baker Academic, 2003), 238.

PART II: Studying Scripture, Question 6, "Our Defiance"

Missions can be defined in various ways. Missions can refer to outreach in foreign countries, cross-cultural contact within one's country, or local community outreach. A mission group may provide humanitarian aid, a combination of mercy ministry and the gospel, evangelism only, or vision and prayer efforts.

[31]   John Calvin, *Commentary on Jonah, Micah, Nahum*, Lecture 79: Jonah.

Lesson 7: The Sovereignty of God

[32]   Saint Augustine, *The Confessions*, Maria Boulding, trans. (Hyde Park, NY: New City Press, 1997), 67.

PART I: Setting the Stage, "Confessions"

The apostle Paul is another example of an esteemed spiritual leader who confessed his sinful heart so that others would not follow his error but turn to God. Paul was an elite Pharisee, a self-righteous persecutor of the early church (Acts 8:3, 9:1; Philippians 3:5-6). After his encounter with Christ, Paul recognized his sinful nature. He realized he could never earn favor with God by his own works (Philippians 3:9) and he confessed he was the worst of sinners (I Timothy 1:15). Grateful for salvation in Christ by God's grace, Paul spent the rest of his life pointing people to Christ.

[33]   Mark D. Futato, *Basic Hebrew*, Lesson 6.

[34]   John Calvin, *Commentary on Jonah, Micah, Nahum*, Lecture 78: Jonah.

Lesson 8: Jesus and the Sign of Jonah

[35]   PART I: Setting the Stage, "Miracles and God's Providence"

God is the uncaused First Cause of all that happens. He may use second causes such as natural forces but He is free to work without, above, and against second causes. The *Westminster Confession of Faith*, Chapter 5, speaks of God's providence: "God, the great Creator of all things doth uphold, direct, dispose, and govern all creatures, actions, and things, from the greatest even to the least." http://www.ccel.org/ccel/anonymous/westminster; Public Domain.

[36]   PART II: Studying Scripture, Question 1, "Signs of the Kingdom of God"

Christians hold various views about the timing of Christ's return in relation to His millennial reign in Rev. 20:4. Four major views are amillennialism, post-millennialism, historic premillennialism, and dispensational premillennialism. This study agrees with the amillennial view that the millennium is not a literal future thousand-year period, but the period between Christ's first and second comings; thus we are currently in the millennium of Christ's reign. The kingdom of God has already come (Luke 4:17-21; Matt. 12:28-29) although not yet in full (Matt. 6:10). God's kingdom will be consummated at the end times when Christ returns in glory. For further study see Anthony A. Hoekema, *The Bible and the Future* (Grand Rapids, MI: William B. Eerdmans Publishing Company, 1979).

[37]   Nancy Pearcey, *Total Truth: Liberating Christianity from Its Cultural Captivity* (Wheaton, IL: Crossway Books, 2005), 91; www.crossway.org.

[38]   Lee Strobel, *The Case for Christ: A Journalist's Personal Investigation of the Evidence for Jesus* (Grand Rapids, MI: Zondervan, 1998), 60.

PART II: Studying Scripture, Question 6b, "The Evidence Today"
The manuscript evidence for the New Testament is much stronger than for any other ancient writing. Although there are no original manuscripts of the New Testament in existence today, the oldest fragment (from the Gospel of John) was copied only a few years after John wrote the original. There are over 5,000 existing ancient Greek manuscript fragments of the New Testament. When these fragments are compared with each other there is little variation, indicating they are extremely accurate copies of the originals.

The closest competitor is Homer's *Iliad,* but the evidence for *Iliad* does not even come close to the mountain of evidence for the New Testament. There are no originals of *Iliad* in existence today. The oldest fragment was copied about 1,000 years after Homer wrote the original around 800 B.C. There are fewer than 650 existing ancient Greek manuscript fragments of *Iliad,* compared to the New Testament's 5,000.

[39]   John Calvin, *Commentary on Jonah, Micah, Nahum,* Lecture 80: Jonah.

Lesson 9: Habakkuk's First Complaint
[40]   John Calvin, *Commentary on Habakkuk, Zephaniah, Haggai,* Lecture 106: Habakkuk; http://www.ccel.org/c/calvin; Public Domain.

[41]   Joni Eareckson Tada, "Dispelling the Smog," excerpted from Joni and Friends Radio Program #8249 broadcast on December 12, 2013, ©Joni Eareckson Tada. Used by permission of Joni and Friends, PO Box 3333, Agoura Hills, CA 91376. Website: www.joniandfriends.org/radio.

[42]   John Calvin, *Commentary on Habakkuk, Zephaniah, Haggai,* Lecture 106: Habakkuk.

[43]   John Calvin, *Commentary on Habakkuk, Zephaniah, Haggai,* Lecture 107: Habakkuk.

Lesson 10: Habakkuk's Second Complaint
[44]   PART II: Studying Scripture, Question 1a, "God's Sovereignty"
The title LORD in capital letters represents Yahweh (YHWH), the covenant name for Israel's God. The true pronunciation of YHWH has been lost since there were no written vowels in ancient Hebrew. Jews considered the name YHWH too holy to pronounce out loud so they instead said Adonai (Lord) when reading YHWH. The vowel sounds of Adonai became associated with YHWH, yielding the name Jehovah. Today the preferred pronunciation of YHWH is Yahweh.

Yahweh means "I AM": God is uncreated and self-existent.
Elohim means God: God is the Creator and therefore Lord over creation.
Holy One of Israel: God is holy, other, transcendent, and perfect.
Rock: God is near, mighty, strong, a refuge, and our protector King.

[45]   R. B. Kuiper, *The Glorious Body of Christ* (Edinburgh: Banner of Truth Trust, 2006), 90; www.banneroftruth.co.uk.

PART II: Studying Scripture, Question 2c, "God's Remnant"
The prophets foretold that God, by the Messiah, would restore a faithful remnant of Israel to their land after the Babylonian Exile. Short-term fulfillment occurred when Jewish exiles returned to Jerusalem and rebuilt the Temple. More glorious messianic fulfillment began at Christ's first coming and will be completed at His second coming. The promises to national Israel have been inherited by the church, which is the true spiritual Israel, the true remnant (Romans 9:6-8).

[46]   O. Palmer Robertson, *The Books of Nahum, Habakkuk, and Zephaniah,* The New International Commentary on the Old Testament (NICOT) (Grand Rapids, MI: William B. Eerdmans Publishing Company, 1990), 162-3.

[47]   PART II: Studying Scripture, Question 4a, "The Wicked: Idolatry"
Other notable Babylonian gods were Nebo (Marduk's son), Sin (the moon god), Shamash (the sun god), and Ishtar (goddess of love and war).

[48]   D. A. Carson, *How Long, O Lord?* (Grand Rapids, MI: BakerBooks, 1990), 151.

[49]   Nancy Leigh DeMoss, *Revive Our Hearts,* "Habakkuk: Hearing From God," Radio Program broadcast on October 13, 2010; http://www.reviveourhearts.com. Used by permission.

[50]   John Calvin, *Commentary on Habakkuk, Zephaniah, Haggai,* Lecture 109: Habakkuk.

Lesson 11: The Justice of God
[51]   Greg L. Bahnsen, *Always Ready* (Nacogdoches, TX: Covenant Media Press, 1996), 172.

[52]   John M. Frame, *The Doctrine of God* (Phillipsburg, NJ: P & R Publishing, 2002), 171-173.

[53] Herman Ridderbos, *Paul: An Outline of His Theology* (Grand Rapids, MI: William B. Eerdmans Publishing Company, 1975), 172, 176.

[54] PART II: Studying Scripture, Question 2a, "God's Righteous One"
Christ's righteousness does not infuse us, but is imputed to us (credited to our record). When God looks at us He sees Christ's righteousness instead of our sinful nature. There is actually double imputation, for our sin is imputed to Christ.

[55] Martin Luther, *Preface to the Letter of St. Paul to the Romans;* http://www. ccel.org/ccel/luther/prefacetoromans; Public Domain.

[56] John Calvin, *Commentary on Romans,* Romans 1:17; http://www.ccel.org/c/ calvin; Public Domain.

[57] PART II: Studying Scripture, Question 4, "Babylon's Doom"
God's grievances against Babylon could be summarized as follows:
Wealth gained by plunder, violence, bloodshed, and heavy taxation (2:6-8).
Wealth gained by stolen materials; economic security at others' expense (2:9-11).
Ruthless pursuit of glory and fame (2:12-14).
Disregard for human dignity; sexual immorality (2:15-17).
(Note that gazing upon nakedness can mean participation in sexual activity.)
Idolatry (2:18-20).

[58] Bill T. Arnold and Bryan E. Beyer, *Readings from the Ancient Near East,* "Epic of Gilgamesh" (Grand Rapids, MI: Baker Academic, 2002), 66.

[59] John Calvin, *Commentary on Habakkuk, Zephaniah, Haggai,* Lecture 110: Habakkuk.

Lesson 12: Habakkuk's Prayer of Faith
[60] *Westminster Shorter Catechism,* Answer 1; http://www.ccel.org/ccel/ anonymous/westminster; Public Domain.

[61] Matthew Henry, *Commentary on the Whole Bible,* Vol. IV, Habakkuk 3:16-19; http://www.ccel.org/ccel/henry; Public Domain.

PART II: Studying Scripture, Question 5d, "Habakkuk's Faith in God"
The approaching invasion by the Babylonians meant devastating loss of essential food, clothing and shelter for Judah. Habakkuk's joyful faith is remarkable in the face of the losses represented in his song:

Fig trees and vines= Fruit, grapes, wine (important when water was scarce)
Olives = Oil (important for cooking and baking)
Fields and crops = Grain, vegetables, material for shelters, food for animals
Herds and flocks = Milk, butter, cheese, meat, leather, wool

[62]   John Calvin, *Commentary on Habakkuk, Zephaniah, Haggai,* Lecture 115: Habakkuk.

Appendix B: Leader's Guide
[63]   Dennis Bennett, "How We Teach and How They Learn," *Equip to Disciple,* Series of ten articles (Lawrenceville, GA: Presbyterian Church in America, 2009-2011); http://www.pcacdm.org/archives.